The Rise of the Labour Party, 1893-1931

The Rise of the Labour Party, 1893–1931

Gordon Phillips

ROUTLEDGE

London and New York

First published 1992
by Routledge
11 New Fetter Lane, London EC4P 4EE

Simultaneously published in the USA and Canada
by Routledge
29 West 35th Street, New York, NY 10001

Reprinted 1994

© 1992 Gordon Phillips

Printed in Great Britain by
Clays Ltd, St Ives plc

British Library Cataloguing in Publication Data
Phillips, Gordon
The rise of the Labour party, 1893–1931. –
(Lancaster pamphlets)
I. Title   II. Series
324.2410709

Library of Congress Cataloging in Publication Data
Phillips, G. A. (Gordon Ashton)
The rise of the Labour party, 1893–1931 / Gordon Phillips.
p. cm. – (Lancaster pamphlets)
Includes bibliographical references.
1. Labour Party (Great Britain) – History.
2. Great Britain – Politics and government – 1837–1901.
3. Great Britain – Politics and government – 1901–1936.
I. Title.   II. Series.
JN1129.L32.P48 1992
324.24107'09 – dc20   91–28658

ISBN 0–415–04051–5

Contents

Foreword

Lancaster Pamphlets offer concise and up-to-date accounts of major historical topics, primarily for the help of students preparing for Advanced Level examinations, though they should also be of value to those pursuing introductory courses in universities and other institutions of higher education. Without being all-embracing, their aims are to bring some of the central themes or problems confronting students and teachers into sharper focus than the textbook writer can hope to do; to provide the reader with some of the results of recent research which the textbook may not embody; and to stimulate thought about the whole interpretation of the topic under discussion.

At the end of this pamphlet is a list of works, most of them recent or fairly recent, which the writer considers most important for those who wish to study the subject further.

Chronology

1893	Foundation of the Independent Labour Party.
1896	ILP proposed co-operation for electoral purposes with TUC and Fabians.
1899	Resolution of the Trades Union Congress to hold a conference with other labour and socialist organizations on parliamentary representation.
1900	Foundation of Labour Representation Committee.
1900	General Election (September–October): LRC wins two seats.
1901	First Taff Vale decision upheld by House of Lords, exposing trade unions to financial penalties for offences arising out of strike activity.
1902–3	LRC gains three more parliamentary seats at by-elections.
1903	LRC establishes political fund and compulsory financial levy on affiliates.
1903	LRC secretary, Ramsay MacDonald, negotiates a secret electoral understanding with the Liberal party whip, Herbert Gladstone.
1906	General Election (January–February): LRC wins 29 seats. Alters name to Labour party.
1907	Labour party introduces its first 'Right to Work Bill'.
1908	Arthur Henderson succeeds Keir Hardie as chairman of Parliamentary party.

1908	Miners' Federation of Great Britain ballots in favour of affiliation to Labour party.
1909	Osborne judgment, upheld by House of Lords, declares the illegality of diverting trade union funds to the support of the Labour party.
1910	General Election (January). Labour party representation falls from 45 to 40.
1910	George Barnes succeeds Henderson as party chairman.
1910	General Election (December): Labour party wins 42 seats.
1911	Ramsay MacDonald succeeds Barnes as party leader.
1913	Trade Union (Political Levy) Act, allows unions to give financial support to the Labour party, through separate political funds approved by their membership.
1914	Outbreak of war. MacDonald resigns as party leader, succeeded by Arthur Henderson. Creation of War Emergency Workers' National Committee by party and trade unions.
1915	Labour party joins the first (Asquith) Coalition government.
1916	Lloyd George succeeds Asquith as Prime Minister. Labour party secures increased Cabinet representation.
1917	Arthur Henderson resigns from the Cabinet, and gives way as party leader to William Adamson. Begins work on a new party constitution.
1918	Representation of the People Act, enfranchises all adult men over 21 and women over 30.
1918	Labour party approves its first national programme, *Labour and the New Social Order.*
1918	Labour party withdraws from Coalition government at the Armistice, and fights General Election independently (December). Gains 59 seats, increased to 63 by subsequent adhesions.
1920	Labour party joins with TUC in the Council of Action, to resist British military involvement in Russia.
1921	J. R. Clynes replaces Adamson as party chairman.
1922	General Election (November). Labour gains 142 seats.
1922	Ramsay MacDonald elected leader of the Parliamentary party.
1923	General Election (December). Labour wins 191 seats.
1924	Labour party forms minority government, dependent on Liberal support.

1924	Labour government resigns. General Election (October). Labour strength reduced to 151 MPs.
1926	General, or National, Strike organized by TUC General Council.
1927	Trade Union and Trade Disputes Act, allows unions to levy contributions for political purposes only with the explicit assent of individual members.
1928	Labour party approves new political programme, *Labour and the Nation*.
1929	General Election (May). Labour, with 288 seats, forms second minority government.
1930	Oswald Mosley resigns as junior minister over the failure of the government to tackle unemployment effectively.
1931	Labour government resigns through inability to agree on budget economies. MacDonald made head of a National Government, including Liberals, Conservatives, and three of his ministerial colleagues in the Cabinet.
1931	General Election (October). Labour wins only 52 seats.

1
Introduction: The historical problem

The emergence of the Labour party confronts the historian with a number of problems. The first is to account for the creation of a new and separate party to represent labour. Who felt it necessary to establish such a political organization, and why? In answering this question we must, of course, consider the timing of the enterprise: what particular conditions prevailed at the birth of the Labour Representation Committee in 1900 and what had delayed its introduction at an earlier juncture?

Britain had acquired a substantial working-class electorate with the enactment of the second parliamentary reform bill in 1867, and this had been enlarged by a further widening of the suffrage in 1884. Prior to the turn of the century, however, the mass of enfranchised wage-earners had not been attached to a separate party. A few radicals associated with the International Working Men's Association (the First International) had called for the establishment of a Labour party in 1872, but to no avail. Some socialist organizations, notably the Social Democratic Federation, had since the 1880s sought to make themselves the political representatives of the working class, but they had attracted only a miniscule following. In Britain, indeed, socialist parties proved much less popular, in the late nineteenth century, than in Germany, France and Italy. Though Britain had, by number or ratio, a larger industrial and urban population than any other European country, these manifestations of social change had not brought any comparable political transformation.

Once a British Labour party had been formed, however, it grew —

1

with great rapidity. This apparent success presents the second of our problems. What factors permitted Labour to advance, within twenty-five years, from a political embryo to a mature party – with the strength and support to form a government, even if only a minority one? Throughout the nineteenth century, third parties had entered the parliamentary scene from time to time, but had never threatened the predominance of the major groupings, the Conservatives on the one side, the Whig/Liberals on the other. Either they had joined with the big battalions, like the Peelites or the Liberal Unionists; or, like the Chartists, they had failed to sustain their challenge. In displacing the Liberals as the principal alignment of the left in British politics, therefore, the Labour party accomplished a quite exceptional feat. Whether its advance owed most to its own assets, to the avoidable blunders of the Liberals, or to unalterable movements of social and cultural change, is an issue that has prompted much historical argument.

Once it had secured office, in 1924, the Labour party was called on to fulfil an unfamiliar task. Now it had not just to improve its organization and gather electoral support, but also to implement its policies and discharge the functions of government. This it attempted with obvious lack of success. Particularly when it returned to power in 1929, it was forced to deal with national economic difficulties which it proved unable to overcome. How and why it failed, as a government, poses a third problem. On this question, too, historians have disagreed, and continue to do so. They are, on the other hand, much more at one in assessing the political consequences of Labour's failures in office. In 1931 came a schism in the party, and a disastrous electoral defeat. It thus checked, and temporarily reversed, the progress in the party's fortunes which had been almost unbroken since its foundation in 1900. It left the movement with the burdens of rebuilding support, renewing leadership and learning the hard political lessons of exercising power over a vulnerable economy in an unsettled world. Its response to these demands can be said to carry us into a different phase of Labour's history.

2
The formation of the
Labour Representation Committee

The franchise measures of 1867 and 1884 created many working-class voters. The suffrage was, of course, denied to women, and it did not include all men. In practice, it gave votes to the majority, but not all, of those who were heads of households, and excluded the majority, but not all, of the rest. Probably no more than three in five of adult male wage-earners were eligible to vote in the elections of the early twentieth century, and the proportion fell well below this in the poor, central districts of large towns. Notwithstanding such inequalities, however, in at least some parliamentary constituencies a considerable majority of the electorate was made up of industrial or agricultural wage-earners. Henry Pelling, in his study of the elections of 1886–1910, identifies 89 such seats in England and Wales; there were probably over 100 throughout Britain, and in many more, the working class comprised at least half of the registered voters.

A system of government had thus been established in which wage-earners could, if they acted in unison, convert their weight of numbers into political influence. At least a measure of such unity was fostered by their social situation – by the fact that they worked together in industrial establishments and lived together in distinctive neighbourhoods. Yet we must be careful not to exaggerate this social cohesion. Large-scale industrial firms remained much less common than small and private enterprises with under one hundred or so employees; while working-class neighbourhoods were diverse and fluid in character. One sign of the lack of class cohesion was the

3

limited membership commanded by the voluntary associations which workers had created for themselves, and especially of the trade unions. (Only one in ten adult men in manual occupations belonged to a union in 1888, and even in 1914 the ratio was no higher than about one in three.)

It is true, of course, that the leaders of quite small organizations of this kind might hope to cultivate the political support of a body of working people wider than their own membership. But this does not alter the fact that electoral reform had not, in itself, sufficed to enable working men readily to enter parliament, or to form an effective party acting in their name and interest. Finance represented an obstacle to success on either count. MPs were not paid an official salary until 1911. Previously, those without an independent income had to combine politics with a remunerative occupation. The first Labour Members had either to depend upon a trade union to support them, or to earn a living by journalism. At least until the corrupt practices legislation of 1883, moreover, elections were apt to impose a large financial burden upon candidates, which working men could clearly not afford. Elections thereafter remained costly affairs, though much of the money had now to be found by party organizations. The electoral system itself constituted another barrier. Working men, even when eligible to receive a vote, had to be placed upon the electoral register, and this might be a complicated matter. If they lived in lodgings, or moved house, or received poor relief, they were liable to be denied a vote or deprived of it. Local party machines played a vital role in ensuring that their own supporters gained and retained the franchise. A new party had to compete with the political engines, large and powerful especially in urban areas, which Tories and Liberals had already constructed.

The leading trade unions were extensive and wealthy enough not to be deterred by these difficulties. But they were not willing to make large sacrifices to achieve political representation. Since the end of the 1860s, they had from time to time displayed a wish to secure entry into Parliament for 'labour' spokesmen, and set up national bodies for this purpose. The Labour Representation League was founded in 1869, the Labour Electoral Association in 1886, but neither body obtained the substantial and wholehearted backing of the movement. The larger unions, particularly the miners, preferred to adopt their own candidates. But whether acting alone or together, the unions were unwilling to engage in an electoral contest unless they could secure approval of their nominees from a local party association – almost always looking to

4

the Liberals. They were reluctant to assume the entire responsibility for running and maintaining their own chosen candidates, still more those of other trades.

As a result of electoral conditions and of their own caution, the unions thus accepted a political dependence on the Liberal party. Karl Marx complained in 1872 that 'almost every leader of English working men was sold to Gladstone, Morley, Dilke and others'. The number of such 'Labour' men who entered the Commons was effectively determined by Liberal wishes: there were only eight so designated at the end of the 1880s. These MPs were expected to give loyal support to Liberal causes and administrations, and were conventionally known as 'Lib–Labs'. Even so, we should not regard their appearance in the Commons as insignificant. Their present did indicate the desire of the trade unions, clearly expressed if tentatively pursued, to be represented by their own men. These organizations of labour no longer thought that middle-class radicals, alone, could adequately express the opinion and interest of their movement. The 'Lib–Labs' were a distinct group within the parliamentary Liberal party, because they were working-class trade unionists, and because they had a special knowledge of and concern for labour questions. They asserted their right to dissociate themselves from the Liberal party on such questions. The Lib–Labs, asserted one of their principal spokesmen, Henry Broadhurst, stood for 'a system by which you cordially co-operate with your friends, while reserving to yourself, should need arise, your own independence of action'. They were not the product of class conflict, for they believed that the interests of working men could be advanced within the existing party and political framework. But they were none the less class-conscious, aware that their experience of life, and hence their views and sympathies, were different from those of most parliamentarians. It was therefore natural that they, and the union movement from which they sprang, should want their numbers to grow.

During the 1890s, the political alliance between the trade unions and the Liberal party was gradually eroded. It was weakened, in the first place, by the growth of socialism. In 1893 a new socialist party was established: the Independent Labour Party. Ideologically less rigid than some of its predecessors, especially the Social Democratic Federation, the ILP set out deliberately to recruit support within the unions. Furthermore, some of its leaders, notably Keir Hardie, deliberately embraced the strategy of a 'labour alliance'. By this term they meant an arrangement under which socialists would join with trade unionists, even where the latter did not profess socialism, in order to support candidates at parliamentary and local elections. Hardie wrote in 1897:

> It must be evident to everyone that no labour movement can ever hope to succeed in this country without the co-operation of the trade unions. . . . Some of us have held the opinion from the beginning that it was possible to make trade unionism and ILPism interchangeable terms for electoral purposes.

The outcome of such an alliance would be a distinct working-class party which, though not committed to socialist objectives, would at any rate be independent of the Liberal and Conservative parties. The ILP, in short, set itself both to make converts to socialism where it could, and to coax the trade unions away from 'Lib-Labism'.

The ILP did not have a large membership. Just over 10,000 paid contributions in 1895, and this number was almost halved by 1901. The party was strongest in Lancashire, Yorkshire and central Scotland, but had only pockets of support elsewhere. Though still larger than the Social Democratic Federation, whose total membership in 1902 stood at around 1,700, it was quite unable to win mass support. On the other hand its propaganda, and that of other socialist missionaries and media, extended much more widely than these membership figures suggest. Socialist newspapers like the *Labour Leader* and the *Clarion*, and many others of a more local character, were read by non-members. The most famous socialist tract of the period, *Merrie England*, written by a *Clarion* journalist, Robert Blatchford, and produced in a penny edition, sold about one million copies during the 1890s. The socialist movement thus consisted of a small core of active enthusiasts (though even this nucleus was constantly in flux), surrounded by a more nebulous body of listeners and sympathizers. Accordingly, while the ILP's parliamentary candidates had no immediate success in winning seats, they were able to muster respectable levels of electoral support – well above what the SDF could achieve. In the election of 1895, 28 seats were fought and an average vote of 1,500 obtained.

This record showed that the party was able to win some backing from trade unionists. It was successful in obtaining a foothold within the union leadership, so that by the late 1890s there were few major unions which did not have at least a handful of socialists on their executives. In several cases, the chief officers could be claimed for the faith. How and why this influence had been gained is a complex story, but it is clear that socialist ideas had a strong appeal for the

6

kind of self-educated, earnest, combative and ambitious man who was naturally drawn into union government. At any rate, Hardie's campaign for a labour alliance had, by the end of the decade, acquired a good deal of support within the union hierarchy.

This support was not sufficient, however, to account for the decision of the Trades Union Congress, in 1899, to set up another body for the purpose of promoting the representation of labour. The socialists were still far too weak to control the TUC. The trade unions evidently had their own reasons for wanting to increase their parliamentary presence, without regard to socialism. In part, their aspirations were fostered simply by the rise in their membership. The years after 1889 saw a rapid burst of recruitment. 'New' unions were established, which embraced hitherto unorganized groups of workers, some relatively unskilled and others possessed of skills not previously recognized. The older unions, including miners, textile workers and engineers, advanced less dramatically but more consistently. Taken as a whole, the union movement organized about three-quarters of a million workers in 1888, but doubled in size by 1892, and reached a strength of over two million by 1900. The demand for the parliamentary representation of the organized working class, which had been voiced since the 1860s, grew louder as this expansion proceeded. More unions had the resources to engage in political activity; more union officials came to entertain ideas of a political career. One indication of this was the increasing number of trade unionists, who, under various labels, successfully contested local elections. By 1896 about 600 were sitting on a variety of councils, boards and other local authorities in British cities. Yet the number of Lib–Lab MPs rose only slowly, from eight in 1889 to eleven in 1898. The discrepancy would become even more obvious in 1900, when four of them lost their seats.

The unions had more specific purposes in view when they entered the political arena. Their interest in local government stemmed from the importance of town councils as employers of labour. Municipalities took over the running of various services like gas and road transport in the late nineteenth century, and the more labour nominees were elected, the greater the pressure on them to ensure good conditions of work. 'The Corporations', one Labour candidate was reported as saying in the Preston municipal elections in 1906, 'were large employers of labour, and he would use all legitimate means to make the corporate body model employers.' As for Parliament itself, the unions increasingly expected it to pass protective industrial legislation. The enactment of shorter hours

7

of work in the mines or on the railways, the compensation of workers maimed or injured at their workplace, better provision for the elderly unable to retain employment or sustain earnings, and to some extent the adoption of public measures to combat unemployment, were all matters which had come to concern the union movement in the 1880s and 1890s. This kind of welfare programme was dear to the socialists, but some items were approved by thoroughly 'Lib–Lab' organizations.

Finally, all unions were interested in the laws which governed their everyday activities. In 1875 Disraeli's ministry had put through legislation which seemed to allow trade combinations to declare strikes without fear of legal reprisals. In the 1890s, however, the courts began to curtail this immunity, by pronouncing that certain forms of stoppage were not to be permitted. Unions were not allowed, for example, to attack employers who had no direct part in the original dispute. The use of pickets to bolster stoppages was also inhibited. The appreciation that the law relating to union activities might require revision and clarification, highlighted the need for additional MPs to put the labour view.

To trade unionists, socialist and non–socialist, the potential benefits of increasing their representation on the elected organs of government were evident. And if they failed so to reinforce themselves, there was a danger that their influence would be outweighed by that of employers. Union leaders were apprehensive about the growth of combinations among capitalists in the 1890s, even though these organizations of masters were largely a response to their own success. In a number of industries, notably engineering and building, alliances of employers had initiated or widened trade disputes, with the intention of containing or destroying labour's power. Against this background, the legal reverses of the decade looked more alarming. Trade unionists felt a marked anxiety that the industrial co-operation of employers betokened a corresponding extension of their political influence. Such fears were unreal, but not unreasonable: larger numbers of industrialists had indeed been entering the House of Commons since the 1870s, even if they formed no coherent political force there. It was natural that labour should wish to secure its own position at Westminster.

Yet while the union movement recognized the need for more MPs of its own class, it was increasingly apparent that such representatives could not be furnished by the old method of co-operation with the Liberals. In the first place, the Liberal party was patently unwilling to adopt parliamentary candidates from

8

a working-class background. The objections arose, not from the party's national organizers, but from its constituency associations, usually dominated by a middle-class clientele, and preferring to put forward someone who had money to spend on elections and other political activities. The future Labour party leader, Ramsay MacDonald, had himself been disappointed in his attempt to secure nomination as a Liberal candidate. But by 1894 he complained of 'a national policy which is compelling what was once the advanced wing of Liberalism to sever itself from an old alliance and form itself into an independent Labour party'.

In the second place, the trade unions could no longer work through the Liberal party without dividing their own forces. Such continued collaboration would inevitably offend the socialists who were so essential to their vitality. It would weaken the active support they could draw on when conducting elections, and might well bring them into competition with the ILP. In some constituencies, during the 1890s, Lib–Labs and socialists were already appearing as rivals. Even trade unionists who were not socialists could see that this was an undesirable state of affairs, calculated to deny success to both candidates. The 'labour alliance' advocated by Hardie, though it entailed independence from the Liberals, offered a simple and sensible escape from this impasse.

It is significant, however, that this shift towards political independence by the labour movement occurred when the Liberals were out of power. After Gladstone's retirement as premier in 1894, his party had entered a period of internal dissension. It was heavily beaten in the election of 1895, and there seemed no prospect of its recovering a parliamentary majority in the foreseeable future. It could thus do little practically to further the interests of the unions, whether in the field of labour law or social policy. The latter might well have felt that they had nothing to lose by setting up their own electoral organization. At the same time, they probably did not expect this strategy to have any marked results unless the Liberals gave it some assistance, by allowing labour candidates to contest certain constituencies where no Liberal was in the field. Even the ILP had entertained hopes of an arrangement of this kind in 1898–9. For labour men, in other words, one of the benefits of 'independence' was to establish a strong bargaining position *vis-à-vis* the Liberal party, and thereby to be allowed to fight the Conservatives in its stead.

In 1899, therefore, the TUC eventually passed a resolution in favour of the establishment of a Labour Representation Committee, to which unions, socialist societies and co-operatives might all affiliate. In a sense, it thereby accepted the principle of an independent electoral alliance to act on behalf of labour. But the resolution still succeeded only because it demanded so little. It did not, for instance, commit the unions to supply financial aid to this organization (resolutions in favour of such a political levy had been defeated in 1897 and 1898). It did not commit the TUC as a whole to support such an organization, but left the decision to individual member bodies. Even so, some of the most powerful of the unions, notably the miners and the cotton textile workers, felt such dislike of socialists that they voted against the proposal. And while the majority of unions, both 'new' and 'old', were prepared to support it, they remained very uncertain as to whether this new experiment would prove successful.

3
The consolidation of the party, 1900–6

The organization formed in February 1900 was weak and impoverished. It had only 187,000 affiliated members in May. Even the unions which had voted for its formation in 1899 were in some cases slow to attach themselves. The new party of labour seemed to represent only a small and marginal element of the labour movement as a whole. It began life without accommodation or paid officials. A general election followed immediately after its inauguration, for which it had no chance to prepare. In the middle of the Boer War, labour and domestic issues were not easily given prominence, while the merits of the war itself engendered some disagreement in the labour movement. The LRC managed to bring forward fifteen candidates at the polls, but only two of them were victorious, and entered a Commons where they were still greatly outnumbered by Lib–Labs. Furthermore one of the two, the railwaymen's leader, Richard Bell, ran under Liberal rather than Labour colours. For some two years the banner of independent Labour representation was carried by the solitary figure of Keir Hardie.

This start was not so unpromising as might at first appear. The Labour Representation Committee had fought only a few constituencies in the election, but it had achieved an average poll of over 4,000. This compared very favourably with the results obtained by the ILP in 1895: its twenty-eight candidates had then each attracted only about 1,400 votes. Moreover the LRC already had, or quickly acquired, some of the attributes necessary for

11

success. It was, in the first place, a workable alliance. It combined the moderate socialists of the ILP with unionists who were politically ambitious and increasingly interested in social reform. It had, on the other hand, the good fortune to be relieved of potentially disruptive elements. The co-operative movement, still strongly Liberal in loyalties, declined to join. The Marxist Social Democratic Federation dissociated itself in 1901. The Fabians, cabalistic rather than democratic in character, remained inconspicuous. In addition, the LRC enjoyed the services of Labour's most colourful and gifted orator, Keir Hardie, and its most able political organizer and negotiator, Ramsay MacDonald.

The LRC's rapid growth after 1900 was, however, chiefly the result of the legal decision which appeared to place the trade unions' right to strike in jeopardy. The Taff Vale judgment, named after the railway company which had brought the action and delivered against the principal railway union, was confirmed by the House of Lords in 1902. It awarded compensation to an employer, whose workmen had broken their contracts to go on strike, and damaged company property, as well as arresting its normal business. The railway union was ordered to pay £23,000, although the dispute was begun by a local official acting on his own initiative. It was immediately obvious to other unions that they would be subject to similar financial penalties, whenever a strike involving their members was accompanied by the slightest legal irregularity. There was, in the event, to be no sustained capitalist offensive in the courts; but the fact that a few employers in other industries quickly started similar proceedings was quite enough to spread fear through the union movement.

Many more unions now flocked to join the LRC. Membership increased from 350,000 at the beginning of 1901 to 861,000 by the end of 1902. This large influx consisted entirely of trade unionists; the number of industrial bodies attached to the party rose from 65 to 127 during 1901–2, and they supplied 847,000 of the official membership in the latter year.. Moreover, the Committee now felt strong enough to require them to make a significant financial commitment. Hitherto, it had imposed on its constituents only a nominal contribution of 10s (50p) per thousand members, sufficient to meet routine administrative expenses. Following the example of the Miners' Federation, it increased this rate to 1d a year for each member (raised again to 2d in 1907), with which it could support its own candidates at elections. MacDonald pointed to the importance of the decision.

Hitherto Labour war chests have been left in the possession of the unions which filled them, and were only used for candidates connected with those unions . . . [N]ow we are to have . . . a common fund, and Labour candidates – not necessarily Trade Unionists – run from that fund.

At the same time, the LRC conference imposed a new and stricter discipline upon MPs and parliamentary candidates, forbidding them to give electoral assistance to the members of other parties. The LRC thus underlined its own independence, and incidentally prompted the resignation of one of its original MPs, Richard Bell. It did not, however, forbid its spokesmen to receive assistance from outside: and this was a significant omission.

Out of the public eye, during 1903, the LRC secured a momentous concession from the Liberal party organization. As a result of secret negotiations between Ramsay MacDonald and the representatives of the Liberals, the latter party agreed, in so far as its central office was concerned, to abstain from contesting some fifty seats where a Labour candidate was thought most likely to defeat the Tories. This arrangement was intended to include the Lib–Lab nominees of the miners as well as the LRC; and it did not extend to Scotland. None the less, its terms conferred a priceless gift upon MacDonald's organization. In effect, the LRC was promised the extensive support of Liberal votes to defeat Conservative opponents; and thereby the opportunity to secure a level of parliamentary representation far above what it could hope for if unaided.

The Liberals had reasons of their own for making this concession, but their generosity indicated that they already thought the LRC a formidable affair. It had done sufficiently well in the election of 1900 to suggest that it could take a substantial number of votes from the Liberals. Moreover in 1902–3, it had acquired three more MPs at by-elections, including one, Arthur Henderson, who had defeated a Liberal as well as a Tory opponent at Barnard Castle. In this situation, the Liberal whips knew that their party's candidates in some industrial areas would be anxious to have a deal struck with Labour, lest it be inclined to turn their own working-class supporters against them. In addition, the fact that the LRC now had a considerable parliamentary fund with which to conduct elections gave it a more impressive air. Paradoxically, indeed, the very independence which Labour now asserted, politically and financially, made co-operation with the Liberals easier, by exempting the latter from the cost of running working-class candidates. On the other hand, the negotiations of 1903 could not have succeeded if the Liberals had thought the new party likely to do harm to a Liberal government. It was because the LRC was manifestly not a socialist organization – because most of its affiliates and parliamentary candidates were trade unionists whose political opinions were often indistinguishable from the Liberals' own – that the chief whip felt so complacent.

In the 1906 election, the LRC put forward 50 candidates, whose average vote rose to about 7,500. The party won 29 seats, while a further, unapproved but victorious candidate immediately joined their ranks. Of the 29 victories, 24 were achieved in straight fights with the Conservatives. The willingness of the Liberals to withdraw their candidates, under the terms of the 1903 understanding, thus played a vital part in Labour's success. In these constituencies, Labour received nearly three in five of the votes cast, whereas they obtained less than one in three when a Liberal was in the field. The LRC showed that it could attract support away from Liberal, as well as Tory, opponents, but not normally in sufficient numbers to have any hope of securing seats.

What kind of party had now taken shape and substance? Judging by its MPs, it was overwhelmingly a party of, as well as for, the working class; but it embodied that class in its most respectable and morally worthy garb. Of both its trade unionist and its social- ist representatives, most were earnest, largely self-educated men. Eighteen of them professed themselves to be religious dissenters, and several were also teetotallers. The men who gave them most active assistance in their localities were of the same character. When the ILP had launched a recruiting campaign in London in 1894, it had directed attention primarily to those workpeople 'found in churches and temperance societies who formed the backbone of the labour movement'. It was just this segment of the working class, sober and regular in habit, which had been able for a generation or more to give time to political and union activities, despite the demands of hard manual work; and which possessed the confidence to assert their equality with politicians from a far more privileged background.

Ideologically, the party was less coherent. It was not defined by a socialist (or any other) programme, but most of its MPs would have called themselves socialists, of a kind. And in the years after 1906, party conferences were quite willing to support resolutions proposing the public ownership of one industry or another. For most of them, however – MPs or conference delegates – socialist

14

causes were not matters of great urgency. It was more important for the party to protect and advance the immediate and tangible interests of the working class. In practice, the nature of those interests was primarily determined by the trade union leadership. The priorities of the party had therefore to lie, for example, in the restoration of the legal protection which the Taff Vale judgment had demolished, the improvement of working conditions where these could be affected by government action, and the engineering of a labour market in which wage-earners would be less insecure and enjoy greater bargaining power. This ideological position was sometimes termed *ouvriérisme* in France, and 'labourism' in England. It would thus be misleading to regard the party as divided into socialists and non-socialists. But it was true that some socialists within it wanted to give more attention, with less delay, to radical objectives. And it was also apparent that some trade unionists distrusted the intellectual tastes and refined manners of many of the ILP, especially if they seemed to be claiming a dominant role. These differences of temper and outlook were to become wider in the next few years.

while different views
they all want to help W/C

15

4

The limits of independence, 1906–14

The years after 1906 were difficult ones for the Labour party. The
very magnitude of its success at the election of that year created
expectations among its supporters which it could not fulfil, and
the objectives which it had set itself were found to be in conflict.
Labour wanted to establish its own political identity, to champion
its own causes and policies. It also wanted to sustain its growth and
organizational expansion. But the policies which it approved could
only be effected if they were taken up by the Liberal government,
which had won a commanding parliamentary majority in 1906;
so that the more effective Labour became as a political pressure
group, the more it would seem dependent upon the Liberals.
Much the same was true of its prospects of growth. The new
party had already benefited from a covert understanding with its
radical counterpart. Its further advance seemed to rely upon the
co-operation of the Liberals, but the latter would clearly not be
willing simply to withdraw from more and more seats. On the
other hand, if Labour sought to compete with the Liberals on a
wide electoral front, the latter would fight back, and endanger the
seats which it already held.

These difficulties were not immediately apparent. Between
1906 and 1908, the Labour party did, to some extent, assert
its independence, by taking up issues which were of particular
interest to a working-class constituency. It demanded the reversal
of Taff Vale; it campaigned strongly for public programmes to
remedy unemployment, and to establish the 'right to work'; it

16

sought the amendment of industrial welfare laws, concerned with workmen's compensation, factory conditions or hours of work. On these questions, especially the first, the party could demonstrate that it was fighting its own corner, yet in a manner that was sufficiently pragmatic or popular to extract concessions from the government. The Trade Disputes Act of 1906, which finally restored the unions' right to strike, free from any fear of legal retribution, was based upon a bill drafted by the Labour party in association with the Parliamentary Committee of the TUC, and replaced the version put forward by the Liberal Cabinet. The fact that Labour gained three more seats at by-elections between 1907 and 1909 provides some evidence – at a time when Liberal fortunes were declining sharply – of the party's ability to make an effective appeal on its own behalf.* From 1909, however, the Liberals themselves adopted an ambitious and constructive policy of social reform, embodying such measures as old age pensions, minimum wage legislation, and state insurance for the sick and unemployed. These schemes, and other increases in public expenditure, necessitated the introduction in 1909 of a highly controversial budget, which was rejected by the Conservative majority in the House of Lords. The rights and wrongs of the 'People's Budget', and more particularly the issue of whether the powers of the Lords should be curtailed, dominated the two general elections which took place in 1910. The Liberals remained in office, but without an overall majority in the Commons. They could successfully attack the Lords' veto only with the support of Irish Nationalist MPs; and as the price of their continued backing, the Liberal Cabinet had to bring in legislation giving home rule to Ireland. In short, party politics throughout the years 1909–14 were dominated by measures and arguments which the Labour party had not foreseen, and to which it could make little or no distinctive contribution.

In these circumstances, the Labour party was pushed on to the political sidelines. When constitutional reform or Irish affairs were under discussion, it could only follow in the Liberals' footsteps, and champion their causes. Even in the sphere of welfare, it found itself no longer pressing for its own proposals, but commenting on and reacting to government policies. In consequence, the Labour

* One of these victories, at Colne Valley in 1907, was won by a 'Labour' candidate, Victor Grayson of the ILP, who had not been endorsed by the party. Grayson stood, however, on much the same platform as other Labour candidates, and it seems reasonable, at this stage of his career, to attribute his support to the electoral standing of the party.

movement was more liable to find itself divided over the merits of the government programme. It could not speak with a clear voice either for or against what the Liberals had achieved. Furthermore, the economic issue upon which it had concentrated most of its publicity between 1900 and 1909 – that of unemployment – now receded into the background, as Britain enjoyed an extended period of commercial prosperity lasting until 1914.

Labour continued to seek concessions from the Liberal administration in these years. But it was now concerned to meet its own needs, as a political organization, not to express a wider working-class interest or public opinion. In 1909 another damaging legal decision, the Osborne judgment, was handed down by the courts, prohibiting trade unions from using their general funds to finance the party. Both Labour MPs and party organization were materially embarrassed, or at any rate unable to plan activity which would require substantial expenditure. To rectify the position, the party had to turn to the government. The latter did, eventually, respond, first by introducing the payment of members of parliament in 1911, then, in 1913, by enabling the unions to set up separate political funds for whatever purposes they designated. In the interim, however, Labour had a powerful motive for keeping on the Liberals' right side. Moreover, the legislation which it was urging was not calculated to evoke widespread interest and support. It exposed the party's MPs to the criticism that they were not idealists, but self-seeking political *parvenus*. And there were always critics ready to lay hold of such charges.

Controversy over party strategy surfaced within a couple of years of the successful 1906 election. It threw up two related issues: the commitment of the party to socialism, and its attitude to the Liberal government. For some elements of the ILP, the failure of the party to adopt socialist policies was made worse by its undue devotion to parliamentary activity. They wished to return to a more propagandist form of politics, directed to making converts to the faith, rather than to returning MPs. One of them wrote:

> By the labour alliance the Socialists set out to permeate the trade union ranks. It was a game at which two could play. . . . There is ground to-day [1913] for maintaining that the Labour party is becoming, in fact, whatever it be in name, merely a wing of the Liberal party, like its precursor the Trade Union Group.

In 1911 some of these discontented militants seceded from the ILP to join with the Social Democratic Federation in a new and undiluted

British Socialist Party. The rapid contraction of this organization in the years 1911–14 served as a warning, however, as to the limited appeal of socialist doctrines to a popular audience.

The radical spirits who remained within the Labour party now called instead for a more outspoken attack on the policies of the Liberal administration, and a thoroughgoing effort to contest parliamentary seats on the widest possible front. They came into disagreement, accordingly, with party leaders like Ramsay MacDonald. The latter considered that a Liberal government was properly to be preferred to a Conservative one, and that an indiscriminate electoral challenge would waste resources and endanger protected seats, including his own.

5
Elections and party support, 1906–14

In pursuing its second goal, of gaining new members and new seats, the party was again most successful in the years immediately following 1906. In addition to the by-election victories already mentioned, it won an adherent of vast importance when, in 1908, the Miners' Federation of Great Britain (MFEB) voted to affiliate to it. This gave the party an additional 12 MPs, bringing its total strength in 1909 to 45. It also placed behind it (though not at its own bidding) the resources of the largest union organization in the country, which was to boast over 900,000 members by 1914. It gave a promise of further advances in mining areas, where a strongly working-class electorate formed tightly-knit, independently-minded and sometimes militant communities. With the miners on its side, moreover, the Labour party had no longer anything to fear from the development of a rival organization, exclusively trade unionist in composition and leadership, which hitherto the Lib-Labs (and perhaps the Liberal party) had hoped to institute. It was now certain that any union which sought political representation would do so under the banner of Labour.

This did not, however, mean that all organized miners, or all trade unionists of any other denominations, could be relied upon to vote for Labour. Many retained their attachment to the Liberals – and some of the MFGB politicians who had ostensibly transferred to the Labour party similarly felt no great loyalty to it. Wage-earners who subscribed to a union irregularly or not at all were, of course, a still less reliable body of electors. This was clearly shown by the outcome of the two general elections which took place in January and December

20

1910. Liberal politicians were not now, as far as the Labour party was concerned, in the generous mood of 1903. They were a government in power, fighting for survival. While they were happy to maintain their electoral understanding with Labour, they were also determined to retain as many parliamentary seats as possible under their own control. Hence although sitting Labour MPs were, as in 1906, given a free run against the Conservatives, almost no other candidates from the smaller party were so helped, and without this degree of Liberal recognition, such candidates proved to have no hope of success. In both elections, Labour could only win in a couple of constituencies where Liberals as well as Unionists were standing. The Liberals, on the other hand, took six seats from Labour. The elections clearly confirmed that most voters, including working-class trade unionists, saw the Liberals as a real and effective alternative to Conservatism. In January, the Labour party actually emerged with only 40 MPs, and though it increased its complement to 42 in December 1910, this figure still left it weaker than it had been in 1909.

The electoral situation of the party grew no more satisfactory in the years up to 1914. Where it presented candidates at parliamentary by-elections, they were invariably opposed and worsted by the nominees of the two major parties. Yet more discouraging, Labour itself lost seats, particularly in the traditional Liberal coalfields of the Midlands, which the Liberals themselves showed a wish to reclaim. By the outbreak of the war, the size of the parliamentary party had declined from 42 in December 1910 to 37. Since the affiliation of the miners, seven Labour members had been defeated at general elections and by-elections, and one had resigned from the party rather than submit to the relinquishment of his associations with Liberalism, on which his union now insisted.

This unimpressive rate of progress has been explained in several ways. Some historians have laid much emphasis on the electoral system itself, and particularly on the limited extent of the working-class franchise. Others have stressed the failure of the party to extend its appeal to those strata of wage-earners lying below the relatively secure and respectable membership of the unions and the socialist societies. Others again have shown how, in some localities, even in centres of industry, the power and influence of social elites could undermine the capacity of the working class for political action on its own behalf. Finally, historians interested in the Liberal and Conservative parties in these years have drawn attention to the strength of the opposition to Labour. The Liberal government tried energetically to sustain its electoral support in face of Labour's competition, radical ministers like Lloyd George showing much skill in cultivating their own popular following. Nor should one forget, in this connection, the efforts which the Conservatives were simultaneously making to revive their working-class support. By providing recreational facilities through the Primrose League, by allying themselves with churches and with publicans, by attacking the more unpopular Liberal measures like contributory national insurance, they too could maintain their hold on some industrial areas. These divergent views cannot be further assessed here. They serve, however, to draw attention to the danger of assuming that the Labour party had a kind of automatic claim on the allegiance of working-class voters. The fact that it was a party springing from that class gave it certain political advantages, but this capital should not be overvalued. In the first place, the working class was far from monolithic, socially or economically. Divisions between the high and low paid, the skilled and less skilled, native and immigrant communities, and many others, tended to inhibit the achievement of any political unity. It must also be appreciated that, in numerous and subtle ways, the cultural climate in which that class lived – its popular newspapers and recreations, its family relationships and its traditional moral values – obstructed the emergence of radical political attitudes. Most working people did not subsist in a world of political discussion and debate, and we cannot account for their voting habits by studying the pronouncements of party politicians. The Labour party did not find it easy to persuade workers that they had much to gain by putting its representatives into parliament.

This difficulty was to remain visible even in later years, when its circumstances were in other respects more favourable. Throughout this period, accordingly, it is necessary to keep in mind the great local diversity of political behaviour. The relationships between the Labour party and the working class, and the extent to which it succeeded or failed in mobilizing the industrial population, varied from place to place. Both the nature of the electorate, and the capacity of the party to affect it, can be properly understood only in these different local contexts.

The Labour party had certainly not overcome its difficulties prior to the First World War. What it stood for, in terms of national policies, was not very clear and it appeared to be making no progress in amassing votes or winning parliamentary seats. Yet we must not rush to the conclusion that it was an organization in decline, awaiting rescue by the hazards of war. If we examine its fortunes in a local context, instead of a national one, we find some indications that the

22

party was doing better. Here, Labour was steadily building up its electoral organization. Here there were more seats to be won, in local government, and sometimes against weaker opposition. And here, too, the party had greater success in demonstrating that it was not just 'a wing of the Liberal party'.

The Labour party had continued to improve its organization, up to the outbreak of war. In this respect, it was in a fairly robust state of health. It had established some kind of representative body in many new constituencies: there were 73 such structures in existence in 1906, and 179 by the beginning of 1914. Some of these, like the party organs in London, Glasgow and Liverpool, encompassed large areas, where they sought to co-ordinate the activities of subordinate organizations, and to assist them when necessary. The growth of party machinery of this kind reflected the efforts of Labour's national officials; but it also marked the expansion of its membership across the country. The years after 1910 saw a dramatic advance of trade unionism, similar to that which had given birth to the 'new unions' in 1888–92. The strength of the industrial movement rose from about 2.5 million members in 1910, to 4.1 million by 1914. The party did not receive all these recruits, but its own membership was none the less much reinforced, standing at just over 1.4 million, in 1910, and rising to nearly 2.1 million by the beginning of 1915. All but 33,000 of this total were affiliated by the unions. Labour's financial position was sounder, in consequence, especially after the Osborne judgment had been annulled. The party was able to add to its full-time agents and officers. It had four such senior staff in 1910, seven by 1914, and there were comparable appointments in some individual constituencies. Most important, it was in a condition to run more parliamentary candidates. At the general election pending at the outbreak of war (and cancelled because of it) Labour seemed to be preparing to fight about 150 seats, more than double the number it had ever contested previously. Though still very much a third party, it was now a far more formidable one.

The same verdict is suggested by Labour's performance in local government elections. By 1913, the party was contesting between 13 and 18 per cent of the seats in municipal council elections in England and Wales. In 1906, 374 candidates stood in 118 towns, attracted 170,000 votes and won 91 seats. In 1913, after some fluctuations, Labour presented 426 candidates in 123 localities, gained 233,000 votes and achieved 171 successes. In both years, these estimates include independent socialists from the SDF or BSP – who ran about 50 candidates in 1913. The results were none the

23

Lael did well - shows taking WIC

less impressive, since they excluded both London and Scotland (the latter returning another 59 town councillors in 1913, together with 13 in the counties). In some areas, the base for a Labour takeover from the Liberals had already been laid.

It was easier for Labour to make an impact in local than in national politics. Electoral competition with the larger parties was not always so strenuous. The local government franchise was some-what more extensive than the parliamentary one, conferring the vote on a minority of women ratepayers, and a higher proportion of working-class men. Labour may have benefited from these conditions, though probably not to any large extent. What assisted it more especially, in local politics, was its ability to present a clearer alternative platform than that of the Liberals. In municipal affairs, the latter were, by comparison with their performance at Westminster, often staid and conservative. Labour could offer a distinctive viewpoint, especially in the field of welfare policy, championing such causes as housing reform, the extension of municipal employment and services, the provision of public clinics or school meals. Its readiness to advocate increased expenditure contrasted with the Liberals' frequent preference for economy and retrenchment.

While Labour was making progress on a local front, however, its advance was still very uneven. In some towns it had secured a substantial representation by 1913, in others it was still negligible. It had 20 members of a council of 84 in Bradford, and won 14 out of 48 wards in Leicester. Having only one seat on the Glasgow corporation in 1907, it captured 16 more by 1914. In Birmingham, on the other hand, it had only 8 representatives among 120 councillors, and in Sheffield only 2 among 64. Throughout England and Wales as a whole (excluding London), its strength was heavily concentrated in Lancashire and Yorkshire. At the outbreak of war, more than half its sitting town councillors were to be found in these two counties; in the regions lying south of the industrial midlands, however, it had only occasional pockets of support.

The growth of local constituency organization, and increased success in local government elections, still left the Labour party with much to do to establish itself as a force in national politics. Even in 1914, it was still unable to contest more than one quarter or so of parliamentary seats and in many of these, its organization remained defective. It often rested upon the efforts of local trade union officials, who had other responsibilities to distract them, and upon a small number of socialist enthusiasts who were not interested in the monotonous business of registering and canvassing voters.

24

To improve its electoral prospects, the party needed more workers ready to carry out these tasks. It went some way to acquiring them when, in 1912, it secured the co-operation of the National Union of Women's Suffrage Societies, whose members campaigned on behalf of Labour candidates in return for their pledging support for the enfranchisement of women. But this alliance could make only a limited contribution to the organization of the working-class vote. In general, the party continued to find it difficult to get all its member organizations to pool their resources and combine their manpower for a common purpose. It was usually one or other affiliated body which, in each locality, took the lead and carried the burden of promoting Labour representation. The party's federal constitution stood in the way of closer collaboration.

The future progress of the Labour party thus seemed, in 1914, likely to be slow and piecemeal, rather than sudden and spectacular. It remained, at the outbreak of war, still at an infant stage of development, more than a mere pressure group but less than a mature political party. It had established an independent existence, but not yet met all the requirements which this condition imposed. We can, however, credit it with two, substantial achievements. First, it had made itself, beyond all question, the party of the trade unions. Neither the Conservatives nor the Liberals could any longer maintain, however many working-class votes they attracted, that they represented *organized* labour. For this reason, the Labour party can be said to have formed a political identity of its own, even if it did not yet embrace a distinct programme or ideology. Second, Labour had built up an electoral capacity which placed it in a strong bargaining position in relation to the Liberal party. The source of this strength lay in Labour's threat to contest the constituencies held by government supporters: if it ran 150 candidates at a general election, it would make a Liberal victory almost impossible. The seriousness of this threat had been obscured by the apparent subservience of Labour to the Liberal administration since 1910, but Asquith and his colleagues were well aware of the danger. On at least two occasions in 1912–14, they made tentative advances to reach some kind of new compact, to replace the electoral arrangement made in 1903. Whether the Labour party knew how most profitably to exploit its bargaining opportunities is doubtful. But at least the opportunities had been created, and they were likely to become more obvious with the passage of time. As it was, the realignment of parties and of electors was postponed by the war; and it occurred, eventually, under very different conditions from those prevailing in 1914.

6

War and reconstitution

Four years of total war wrought great changes in British politics. Ultimately, these developments played a critical role in expanding the Labour party, and establishing it as a potential party of government. The effects of the war, however, took some time to crystallize. They were not simply the unavoidable result of military conflict and economic upheaval, but of the choices and responses of politicians. The statesmen of the old parties were confused and uncertain about the long-run significance of the struggles of 1914–18, and spent the next few years attempting to assess and readjust to a new world. Thus we need to take this post-war period, until about 1922, into account in judging the consequences of war. It was only in these post-war years that the Labour party's new-found strength became apparent.

The outbreak of the war had created some disarray in Labour's ranks. Britain's involvement in this European dispute was approved by the majority of the movement, but some, including most members of the ILP, deplored it. The party was thus seriously divided, and its leader, MacDonald, who held to the minority position, resigned in favour of a more patriotic trade unionist, Arthur Henderson. Issues like the adoption of compulsory military service in 1916 continued to cause internal disagreements. In the event, however, the Labour party avoided the lasting split which was to occur in the socialist movements of France and Germany. In the first place those who opposed the war for the most part refrained from openly campaigning against it, and devoted their efforts instead to urging measures for the prevention of future wars. On the desirability of these safeguards, almost all the party could agree. In the second place, patriots and critics alike were united in demanding that the economic welfare of the working class should be defended and protected, even during the national emergency. They were able to co-operate amicably, on bodies like the War Emergency Workers' National Committee, which was created to press for adequate government protection for servicemen's families, the restraint of food prices, rent control and so forth. Third, even those Labour men who endorsed Britain's war effort were often mistrustful of the way in which the governments of Asquith and Lloyd George conducted it. Though the parliamentary party was represented in the government from May 1915, and in the cabinet after Lloyd George came to power in December 1916, it was never wholly at ease in coalition. In August 1917 Henderson resigned from the war cabinet, when the Labour leaders were refused permission to attend an international socialist conference to discuss peace conditions. Thereafter, it was all but certain that the party would withdraw from the coalition as soon as hostilities ceased.

By the time of his resignation, Henderson and his colleagues were the keener to foster party unity, in order to take full advantage of Labour's rising political prospects. What had caused this optimism? One factor was the continued surge of party membership. The unions enjoyed favourable bargaining conditions for much of the war, and their numerical growth was reflected in the new recruits affiliated to the party. Total party membership increased from 2.1 million in 1915 to 3.5 million by early 1919. More important still, however, was the promise of further franchise extension, which was fulfilled in the Representation Act of 1918. This measure increased the size of the registered electorate from some 7 million, as it had stood in 1910, to 21 million: comprising now all men over 21 (whether householders or not) and all women over 30. A considerable majority of these new voters were drawn from the working class, and were at least within Labour's reach.

Two other wartime developments, though more difficult to gauge, also heightened Labour's confidence. A division within the Liberal party had appeared, when Lloyd George displaced Asquith as Prime Minister in December 1916, which had widened thereafter. The Liberal's electoral organization had unquestionably suffered from the resultant ill-feeling and uncertainty. Moreover, a large section of the Liberals now became closely tied to the Conservatives, whose parliamentary support was required to keep Lloyd George in power. The Labour leadership thus saw the opportunity, once the war was over, to establish itself as the principal vehicle of opposition to the government. Though there were risks to this strategy, and though some prominent Labour men held office in the wartime coalition and wished to continue this partnership in peacetime, the policy of independence offered considerable attractions. It meant that Labour could appeal for the support of newly enfranchised voters at a time when the Liberals were in disarray. It meant that the party could expect to win over former Liberal electors who wished effectively to oppose a government dominated by Tories. And it meant that some radical Liberal MPs could be persuaded to defect to Labour – a process already under way during the war years, and persisting in its immediate aftermath.

If we look beyond constitutional reform and party politics, we may detect, more obscurely, changes which the war encouraged in the political culture. The war familiarized the nation with the scope and potential of an omnipresent, interventionist state. Central government involved itself in all spheres of everyday life, as it had never done before. It conscripted men and women, rationed food and other necessities, fixed rents and wages, ran factories; and its enterprises and propaganda filled the newspapers and cinema screens. At the same time, the state announced its intentions to bring in vast and generous schemes of social reform. As a way of maintaining public morale in an exhausting conflict, it gave pledges of the enjoyment of 'reconstruction' to follow, and created a ministry to plan it. In ways which can be discerned only very imperfectly, these developments changed the common perception of politics, or at least accelerated changes that were hitherto undeveloped. For working people, especially, the actual and prospective importance of the state in determining their well-being was obvious. Until 1914, it had remained possible for them to look to their own, autonomous organizations – unions, co-operatives, friendly societies – to provide many of their needs. They could still readily turn to a variety of unofficial, informal and voluntary sources for material help or support: to charities, to employers, to neighbours, to fellow-workers. These associations were not destroyed by the war, but they were disrupted, and perhaps weakened. To this extent, the protection which could be afforded by the state assumed a higher value, and the attractiveness of a political party which would voice their interests in the forum of government, could perhaps itself become a government, was correspondingly increased.

28

We must not exaggerate the change in working-class political attitudes, which was typically slow and incomplete. Some groups of workers, however, had more particular reasons for concern with the conduct of government. The war had, on the whole, brought higher earnings and more secure employment to those wage-earners who remained in civilian life. In some cases, as in coal mining and railway transport, such gains appeared to result directly from the control of industry by the state. Workers in these occupations naturally wished such control to continue, and were drawn to the Labour party as the champion of a policy of nationalization. Other trades had seen alterations less welcome to the workforce, like the recruitment of large numbers of women to carry out routine but essential jobs. The government had promised that such extraordinary employment policies would be reversed when peace returned but their assurances were probably not wholly believed. In these industries – and perhaps among servicemen anxious about a return to civilian life – the threat of unemployment, which had benefited the Labour party in the past, once more became a political issue.

If the war had political consequences from which Labour might stand to benefit, the party had still to show its capacity to exploit them. Its hopes for the future gained expression in a new constitution and a first party programme, both adopted in the course of 1918. Through these, Henderson and his collaborators set out to make Labour a national party, with a clear set of policy objectives and the means of competing for the support of a mass electorate in all types of constituency. It was to become a party on the same scale, and with the same ambitions, as its older rivals.

The 1918 constitution placed the party organization on a new footing. At the centre, it enlarged and reformed the executive. While still representing the different organizations and sections within the party, this was now to be chosen by the aggregate votes of the whole party conference. The nominees of the constituent organizations were, at least in principle, made accountable to the party at large, and rewarded primarily for their efforts in its service. In addition, financial subscriptions were increased, to make provision for a much more extensive machinery, through which to prepare and disseminate policy, to establish a constituency structure and to fight elections. In the localities it created constituency parties. These would still embrace affiliated organizations, like trade union and ILP branches, but they would also, unlike their pre-war counterparts, admit members as individuals.* Men and women could now join the party directly, instead of through an intermediary body. Furthermore, the constitution set out, in broad and somewhat vague terms, the central aims of the party: among them, to advance democratic forms of government, and to place private economic enterprises under public ownership and democratic control.

The programme which accompanied this constitution, *Labour and the New Social Order*, was also collectivist in tendency. It proposed the nationalization of those industries, notably mining and railway transport, which had been under state direction during the war. It also envisaged the public ownership of the insurance system (though not of banking), of electricity generation, and (by stages) of land. The main aims of such collectivist policies were at the outset, to return economic life to conditions of peace, avoiding the dangers of unemployment and falling living standards and, in the longer term, 'to secure the elimination of every kind of inefficiency and waste'. Beyond this, the programme set out a far-reaching scheme of educational and welfare measures, which were to be financed by further instalments of graduated and direct taxation.

The New Social Order thus marked the formal acceptance by the Labour party of a socialist ideology. Its acceptance revealed that the unions had, during the war, become more confident of the advantages of economic regulation by the state. Though they still had their reservations, in general they felt that public enterprises afforded them fuller bargaining rights and better working conditions than private ones. For them, socialism meant primarily a prosperous market for labour, in which industrial organizations would enjoy security and exert substantial power. For Henderson and other party leaders, in contrast, a socialist programme was desirable because of the supposed breadth of its electoral appeal. They wished it to be seen as a national, not just a sectional, statement. Their programme was, as R. H. Tawney put it, 'a forest of Christmas trees with presents for everyone'. They entertained, indeed, rather unreal hopes that it would win support among the professional and managerial middle class – workers by brain as well as workers by hand. Designed to be popular, the programme was accordingly somewhat rhetorical

* Individual recruitment had been permitted in three local parties before 1914, and there had been little obstruction to individual participation in ward organizations. But this happened as a result of local initiative, taken without formal authority.

and woolly. It left unanswered many difficult questions about how socialist policies could be applied in a market economy. It tended to assume, as a matter of faith, that the capitalist economy itself would continue to flourish and prosper. It paid no serious attention to the existence of foreign commercial competition, or to the possible ill-effects of raising taxation.

The new constitution was designed to accommodate those numerous recruits which the programme was supposed to attract. Henderson wished Labour to become a mass party, in which distinctions between socialists and trade unionists would disappear. But his hopes were to be disappointed. The unions continued to provide the party with most of its finance, and could not be denied the right to reserve most of the seats on its executive for candidates whom they nominated. Party conferences remained under the sovereignty of their block votes. The majority of MPs, throughout the 1920s, were sponsored by a trade union, and after 1926 some of them formed a union group in the House of Commons to scrutinize policies and communicate opinions on issues of an industrial character. The Joint Board, set up before the war, was reconstituted in 1921, to allow formal discussions between the party executive, the parliamentary party and the TUC, giving the union leadership another medium through which to influence Labour's policies. Yet the unions established this position not so as to dominate the affairs of the party, but to safeguard their own interests. They maintained the right not only to complete freedom of action in the sphere of industrial relations but, at least in some matters, to formulate their own political aims and opinions. They would never accept that their concerns and those of the party were inseparable. Given a sufficient independence, however, they were content to hold in reserve their power to control the party. They could thus not be said to run the political wing of the movement, but neither were they directed by it. Labour remained a federal organization, and its political conduct necessarily involved the exercise of tactful diplomacy to assimilate its different parts.

The authority of the unions remained, ultimately, unassailable because there was no other element in the party which had comparable numerical and financial strength. The new constituency parties might have provided a counterweight, but they were unable to enlist members on a similar scale. Though supporters did enter the party, through this route, they never constituted more than a fraction of its total affiliated membership. In 1928, the figure had reached 216,000 but the unions still furnished ten times that number. The disparity was usually significantly greater. In 1930, only 47 constituency parties in England and Wales had over 1,000 individual members.

The growth of Labour constituency parties was held back, prior to 1931, because the ILP preserved its status, now decidedly anomalous, as a party within the party. Though it had less importance and influence under the new constitution than in past years, it retained the loyalty of its adherents. During the early 1920s, indeed, it was still expanding, proving more attractive to socialists entering the party than the new constituency organizations. In 1925 the ILP had 1,028 branches throughout the country. These often had much more vitality and dynamism than the official, divisional organizations of the party. In addition, even more than the unions, the ILP asserted its political independence by framing and propagating its own programmes. Its existence was increasingly irritating to a party leadership which wanted unity and disliked criticism, not least because the ideas presented by the ILP were sometimes more radical and exciting than their own.

Labour's reconstitution in 1918 thus did not create an integrated mass party. It did, on the other hand, make possible rapid organizational expansion. The number of local constituency parties (Divisional Labour parties) increased from 239 in 1916 to 492 by the beginning of 1920 and to 529 by 1924. Not all of these followed the specifications laid down in the constitution. Some continued to perform industrial as well as political functions, some had only a handful of members, some continued to serve more than one constituency. None the less, by 1924 there were only 32 constituencies in England and Wales without a local party body of some kind. This expansion was followed by a similar increase in the number of full-time party agents, paid to represent its interests in a particular locality, from 17 in 1912 to 80 in 1918, 113 in 1924, and 169 in 1929. But what illustrates the advance of party organization most clearly is the number of candidates which it put forward at successive parliamentary elections. Having risen fivefold between 1910 and 1918, this figure continued to grow throughout the 1920s.

1918   361
1922   414
1923   428
1924   515

From 1918, therefore, the Labour party did undoubtedly embrace new, active and devoted followers, prepared to work diligently on its behalf: at the centre, intellectuals like Leonard Woolf and Bertrand Russell; in the localities, a host of unrenowned men and women ready to carry on the work of canvassing, collecting and managing. On the other hand, Labour had not become the kind of popular crusade which, in different ways, Chartism and Liberalism had once been. It did not mobilize the working class in large demonstrations and enthusiastic audiences. It failed to establish an effective party press. It tried, but failed, to form the kind of cultural offshoots which had helped the growth of the German Socialist Party. Its principal *raison d'être*, in short, became electoral success; and it was the rise in its vote, and the winning of parliamentary and council seats, which gave it satisfaction and an encouraging sense of political progress.

7

Labour's electoral achievement, 1918–29

The Labour vote in parliamentary elections expanded steadily throughout the first half of the inter-war years. The trend can be recorded in the percentage of the total ballot received by the party at successive elections.

1918   22.2*
1922   29.5
1923   30.5
1924   33.0
1929   37.1

* Including the votes of four unendorsed MPs who joined the party immediately after the election. The estimate of the vote is complicated by the presence of independent socialist candidates.

This advance was paralleled by a similar, though more uneven, pattern in local elections. No country-wide survey of such contests has been published, but Labour's performance in the municipal seats of one of its strongest areas, West Yorkshire, suggests the course and ratio of its gains elsewhere. The list below of the number of seats secured in each annual election shows rapid advances, first in 1919 (under a new and wider local franchise) and then in the period 1926–9.

1913   85
1919   88+
1920   84+

1921	84+
1922	73
1923	82
1924	90
1925	106
1926	129
1927	141
1928	161
1929	157

Note. The figures for 1919–21 indicate the number of seats won following the redrawing of ward boundaries and the enlargement of the local government franchise. The total number of Labour councillors is much larger, since only one third of them retired in any given year.

By the end of the decade, across the country at large, the Labour party controlled 16 of the 80 principal boroughs in England and Wales, excepting London. It is noticeable, however, that this performance changed the pattern seen before the war. Then, the progress which the party made in local elections had been more consistent than its success in parliamentary contests; now, the position was reversed.

To judge how effective Labour was proving as an electoral force, we need to look at some of these results more closely. In a national context, the party had not fulfilled its own expectations at the general election of 1918. It then faced a largely unified adversary, the alliance of Lloyd George Liberals and Conservatives. The results were influenced by other unusual and unhelpful circumstances: a patriotic mood which prevailed against all left-wing candidates who had condemned Britain's war policy, and a low poll among servicemen who might have favoured Labour. Even so, the party was able to establish itself, ahead of 'opposition' Liberals (who received only 12.2 per cent of the popular vote), as the principal opposition to the government in power. The apparently indifferent performance of the party in the local elections of the West Yorkshire conurbation in 1922 and 1923 can be similarly accounted for, by the establishment of hostile electoral alliances of Tories and Liberals. But here, too, though frustrating its ambitions for the moment, such arrangements served to highlight Labour's claim to be the only genuine embodiment of radicalism. Any rupture of these alliances, and any emergence of a protest vote, was almost certain to work to its advantage.

What Labour achieved, broadly speaking, in the post-war years of 1918–24, was the displacement of the Liberals in working-class parliamentary constituencies throughout most of Britain. Having already secured large tracts of the coalfields in 1918, the party proceeded to establish itself in almost all the other urban concentrations in the early 1920s: the Clyde Valley; Tyne and Wear; East London and the textile regions of Lancashire and Yorkshire. By the end of the decade it was making similar inroads in the West Midlands, in other districts of London, and on Merseyside and Humberside. It did not, as we have seen, simply appropriate working-class Liberal voters, for the bulk of its electorate consisted of those newly enfranchised after the war. Labour superseded the Liberals, perhaps in the manner of heirs to a property, by securing the support of the children of Liberal fathers. It is, at any rate, beyond doubt that the geographical areas in which Labour established itself by 1929 had, in very many instances, been dominated by the Liberals in their Victorian and Edwardian heyday.

How are we to account for Labour's electoral progress? Perhaps more than anything it was owed to the party's working-class character – to the ease with which the voters of industrial communities identified with it. Very many of its MPs, and often its leaders too, had experienced the life of a manual wage-earner, and could speak with conviction of the problems and hardships of that condition, as they could understand the attitudes and prejudices which sprang from it. The social complexion of the Labour back-benches is sufficiently indicated by the number of MPs sponsored by the trade unions: of 61 elected in 1918, 50 were so accredited (half of whom were miners), while in 1923 still 102 of the 191 Members remained in this category. Although the proportion continued to fall, it remained substantial; and it was common enough, of course, for local Labour parties themselves to choose candidates from this same social background. In comparison with their Labour opponents, Liberal politicians had, almost without exception, to speak to the majority of their electors across a class divide, in a style and idiom which evoked no natural sympathy. Though the party had established networks of working-men's clubs in urban areas, their clientele had never been readily involved in political activity. As Liberal organization decayed, in the years after 1914, the problem grew harder to rectify.

Labour's advance would clearly have been less rapid, however, if the governments it faced had been more popular, and in particular had earned more working-class approval. But neither the Lloyd George administration of 1918, nor the Conservative ministries of

1922–3 and 1924–9, under Bonar Law and Baldwin, succeeded in stemming the movement of votes to Labour. The Lloyd George coalition, indeed, grew to be cordially disliked by many wage-earners, so that its record does much to explain the subsequent decline of Liberal support in industrial areas. Having promised generous programmes of social reform, notably in education and housing, the government allowed its financial embarrassment and its fear of price inflation to prompt the severe curtailment of these plans. Having raised hopes, too, that the key industries of coal and railway transport would be taken into public ownership, it later, for similar reasons, restored them to private hands. Above all, having presided over a post-war economic boom, it ended its term of office in the midst of a world-wide commercial depression. Though this crisis was its responsibility only in a very limited degree, it was none the less naturally blamed for the resulting distress. The painful cuts in money wages that were almost universal, the large-scale disputes which soured industrial relations, and the rapid rise in unemployment, created much social bitterness. The anxieties about their future which workers had entertained during the war seemed now to be confirmed. Labour was well-placed to exploit the electorate's disenchantment with Lloyd George, and effectively to challenge his colleagues, especially those on the Liberal side, who depended on working-class votes.

The Lloyd George coalition fell from power in 1922. It was, however, not until another two years, and two elections, had passed that Labour's destruction of the Liberals in industrial Britain was complete. What finally resolved this struggle was first the creation, albeit brief, of a Labour government in January 1924 and second the Liberals' own *de facto* withdrawal from the contest at the election which followed. The advent of a Labour administration was of great significance, in part simply because it demonstrated, in a practical fashion, that this untried and unversed party could indeed take on the responsibility of power. The experiment might not have been attended with any very positive success – but it confirmed what was more important, that a Labour ministry did not entail any national catastrophe. The government behaved like a government, handling day-to-day affairs with competence, running departments of state, paying its bills and treating with foreign powers like any of its predecessors. The Liberals, who had hoped that some crisis or folly would cause MacDonald's cabinet to retire in embarrassment and dishonour, were disappointed. Thereafter, they could no longer expect the electorate to conclude that they alone had the capacity to take the reins of government from the Conservatives.

The first Labour government inflicted upon the Liberals a still graver wound. MacDonald was aware that his ministry, with only 191 Labour men in the Commons, could not expect to survive for any length of time. Rather than remain reliant on Asquith to support it, he looked for an early opportunity to fight a new election. Given a pretext, in the autumn of 1924, he appealed again to the country, claiming that a Liberal–Conservative combination had overthrown him. The tactic showed considerable political acumen. It highlighted the inconsistency of the Liberals' political stance, uncertain whether to back a Labour or a Conservative government, yet no longer with any plausible claim to form a government themselves. It also found them, in contrast with Labour, quite unprepared to fight another election. In short, MacDonald had used this opportunity to force the country to choose between a Labour and a Conservative administration, knowing that Labour would lose, but confident that the Liberals would be annihilated. His calculation was entirely justified. Fielding one hundred fewer candidates than in 1923, the Liberals' parliamentary strength fell from 159 to 40, and their proportion of the poll from 29.6 per cent to 17.6 per cent. They were no longer a party contending for office. When their organization and ambitions recovered, in the 1929 election, they found that they were widely regarded as a political irrelevance, equipped with sensible policies but not worth voting for.

8
The nature of Labour's support

By the mid-1920s, as we have seen, Labour had replaced the Liberals as the principal party of the left in British politics. And it had done so, unquestionably, by attracting to itself a far larger working-class vote than it had commanded before the war, or even in 1918. It had secured a wider geographical coverage, thanks partly to its own organizational effort. It had also acquired support among groups within the working class who had earlier remained outside its embrace. But who precisely were its new-found electors and adherents?

In the absence of opinion polls and political surveys, this question is not easily answered. Obviously, however, one such group was made up of working-class women, formerly unenfranchised. Both those employed outside the home and those who came to be called 'housewives' were, after 1918, the targets of party propaganda. The influence of this propaganda is debatable; and it is usually suggested that women voters were far more Conservative than men. On the other hand, it is very likely that Labour received more support among them than did the Liberals, who were thereby more easily overhauled. Furthermore, Labour's greatest electoral triumph of the inter-war period, in 1929, had been preceded a year earlier by the extension of the franchise to women aged between 21 and 30. These younger voters, many of whom were wage-earners, might well have entertained more radical sympathies than their elders.

There is, in addition, better evidence that Labour did attract and enrol women as party members during the 1920s. The Women's

Labour League, which had organized female support before the war, claimed a membership of only 5,500 in 1918; but the party estimated that 200,000 belonged to the women's sections by 1925. This figure may exaggerate the spontaneous influx of women into the party, in so far as it probably includes some trade unionists, in addition to those joining as individual members. Of the latter, no official figures were given until 1933, when female membership stood at 155,000 and male membership at 211,000, but the female influx of the 1920s had clearly been considerable, especially where local parties had established an extensive ward organization that was readily accessible to them. Even in the early 1920s, therefore, Labour MPs were found acknowledging the assistance which women supporters had given to their campaigning. One successful Scottish candidate said of these helpers in 1922: 'They hustled the indifferent to the booths: they lent shawls and held babies: they carried the sick and dying to the polls on mattresses – and they won.'

The Labour party was, of course, fully aware of the need to cultivate women voters. It did something, at least, by way of acknowledging their citizenship. The 1918 constitution allocated four seats on its executive to the new women's sections. The party also appointed women political agents, and included a woman trade unionist, Margaret Bondfield, in the 1924 Cabinet. At the same time, there were clearly limits to its success in gaining and keeping the support of women, as voters or members. Party leaders were apt to assume, both before and after the war, that women had their own distinctive and peculiar interests and aspirations, giving them a separate political identity. Women's sections were expected to concern themselves with these interests, while a Labour women's conference took place annually to discuss issues like health care, child welfare, or voluntary social services. The essentially domestic role of women was not questioned, even if it was desired to stress its political relevance. In general, indeed, the party was inclined to deplore the entry of women, especially married women, into the labour market. The result of such employment, asserted *The Book of the Labour Party* in 1924, would be to 'do injury to themselves, their children and the race'. Many women may have shared this view; but they did not therefore accept the judgement which lay behind it, that political questions affecting working men were of more importance than those affecting women. The trade unions even objected to placing a demand for family allowances or child benefit in the party programme, for fear that male wages would be reduced in consequence. There was little recognition of the fact that,

40

with limited work opportunities and little economic independence, women would be less likely to share the political attitudes of their husbands, and might well regard Labour as a party of the male and not the female of the household.

The party was more successful in broadening its support among male voters of the working class. Before the war, it had centred itself almost wholly in localities with a strong trade union presence. But clearly, at that stage, many trade unionists had remained reluctant to support Labour. After 1918, they were more willing to do so. This shift of loyalty was especially visible in the coalfields, where many miners remained Liberal in sympathy before the war, but voted solidly for the Labour party after 1918. Other organized workers probably moved, more slowly, in the same political direction. This trend was the result of various factors, including the growing popularity of nationalization and the larger part which union leaders were taking in political debate and discussion. Essentially, it indicates the recognition by the union rank and file of the natural and intimate connection between industrial and political combination. They might well be better off if Labour were in power, as they had been during the war when Labour representatives had entered the government. At any rate, they probably felt assured that a Labour administration would not be accompanied by wage cuts and a reduction of welfare benefits.

The Labour electorate of the 1920s, however, came to extend, even among males, well beyond the limits of trade union influence. Union membership reached its peak, of 8.3 million, in 1920. Thereafter it contracted sharply, amounting to only 4.8 million in 1928. By 1929, no more than about two million trade unionists were affiliated to the party, whereas its election poll had increased to 8.3 million. These statistics show, however roughly, the considerable extent of support for Labour candidates among non-unionists. One way of explaining this trend is by reference to the increasing weakness of the unions on the industrial front. High unemployment persisted, from the end of 1920 until the Second World War. For most of this period it was risky, and often futile, for workers to seek to improve conditions by strike action. In the years 1921–3, many of them discovered this from personal experience, when large-scale stoppages of work met with defeat at the hands of employers. The failure of the General Strike in 1926 furnished a similar lesson. Under these conditions, it can be argued, the labour force perhaps sought for a political outlet for their sense of bitterness and frustration; and perhaps saw in the Labour party a means of securing economic

41

objectives, such as shorter hours of work or guaranteed minimum wages, which could not be achieved by industrial movements. Moreover, in a period of depression, workers were naturally more interested in the protection given by welfare legislation than in times of prosperity. Accordingly, they might well find reasons for favouring a party which promised such social reform, especially fairer treatment for the unemployed, while seeing no corresponding advantage in paying union subscriptions.

These are general and hypothetical arguments. In some, more specific instances, however, we can discover additional grounds for the readiness of unskilled workers to transfer their political allegiance to the Labour party. The Irish Catholic communities, who were resident in many British cities, provided one important element in Labour's electorate. Until 1918, they had been firmly attached to the Liberal party, which had since 1886 championed the cause of Irish Home Rule. But the aftermath of the Irish rebellion of 1916 and the rise of Sinn Fein removed the basis of this political alliance. In 1921, the Irish Free State obtained its independence of the United Kingdom, and the erosion of the Liberal Catholic vote was complete. Already Labour was making strenuous efforts, in some areas, to win over the Irish in Britain to its side, partly by advocating the Irish cause in the military struggle which preceded the 1921 treaty, partly by making friends with the Catholics over questions of interest to them, notably education, and partly by enlisting Irish community leaders. These tactics helped Labour to increase its parliamentary representation in Glasgow, where the Irish formed about 20 per cent of the electorate, from one seat in 1918 to ten in 1922. Less spectacularly, they assisted it in other urban constituencies where the Irish were numerous.

Other factors, though more difficult to assess, doubtless contributed to Labour's rising popularity in the 1920s. The establishment of new estates of council housing gave rise to settled and homogeneous working-class communities with a particular interest in this aspect of state and local government activity. The resulting migration from congested and sometimes squalid urban areas was itself one aspect of the general improvement in living standards enjoyed by most wage-earning families during and after the war. This, it seems likely, raised their material expectations, and thus the disposition to give their political allegiance to a party which would defend those higher standards. At the same time, the kind of political influence which, before the war, social superiors had still at times wielded over inferiors – employers over their workpeople, landlords over their tenants, publicans over drinkers – almost certainly diminished. The political parties communicated with their voters directly, and the impact of propaganda and of electoral organization was correspondingly greater.

While all these social trends were favourable to the Labour party, its progress was not unhampered, and must not be exaggerated. Although it had close ties with the industrial working class, and although that class formed a majority of the population, the party could never, in this period, win the support of a majority of the electorate, or even of its working–class element. Thus while it overtook the Liberals in the quest for votes, it remained well behind the Conservatives. Even in 1929, when it won more seats than Baldwin's party, it still received over a quarter of a million fewer votes. In all other elections of the inter-war period the Conservative lead was substantially greater than this.

We can account for the electoral dominance of the Tories, in part, by pointing to their extensive middle-class and rural support. There was, it is true, a fringe of the professional class, and a minority of small business people of humble origins, who were attracted to Labour. MacDonald and Henderson could not however, seriously suggest that their efforts to establish a national party, embracing what Webb called the *nouvelle couche sociale*, had been successful. Moreover Labour remained weak in almost all agricultural constituencies, even though these contained a significant body of wage-earners. Labour indeed did worse in some rural constituencies at the end of the 1920s than they had done earlier. Yet these factors are not sufficient to account for the Conservatives' continued electoral advantage. There were not enough middle–class and rural voters to have this effect; and some of them, in any case, adhered to the Liberals.

There were a good many members of the urban working class, it must be concluded, who gave their votes to the Conservatives. This was probably true in many considerable towns, lacking large-scale industries and union organizations, like Ipswich and Gloucester. It was equally true of some of the newly expanded industrial centres of the period, such as Oxford and Slough. Throughout the south and west of England, indeed, Labour won only a tiny handful of seats, even in urbanized areas. Yet northern towns which lacked such genteel pretensions, like Grimsby and Lancaster, also remained beyond Labour's grasp. In some of the largest cities, too, the allegiance of the working class was very questionable. London was always volatile, but the Conservatives kept much popular support outside the East End, and even in those poor and overcrowded districts there were odd pockets of persistent Liberalism. Birmingham and Liverpool displayed an allegiance to Toryism which was shared by all sections of their communities. In the former, this derived originally from Joseph Chamberlain's opposition to Irish Home Rule in 1886, in the latter it was of much longer standing, but drew likewise on anti-Irish feeling. Labour began to challenge the Conservative hegemony in 1929, when it won six of the twelve Birmingham seats, and four out of eleven in Liverpool. But even this success – which proved very short-lived – left substantial enclaves of working-class Toryism untouched. Across the whole country, indeed, it has been estimated that, even at the height of its fortunes, Labour in the inter-war period never secured more than half of the votes cast by the working class, if we take this to include all those economically dependent upon wages. Only in a very partial way was it labour's party.

We have already noticed, in considering the politics of the pre-war period, the several reasons offered to explain why so many workers remained indifferent to Labour's appeal, and gave more or less casual electoral support to the older parties. One of these explanations – the limitation of the franchise – ceases to be relevant in the inter-war years. But the other, sociological and cultural, handicaps suffered by the Labour party were still manifest. Politics now seemed a little more significant to the well-being of families and communities; but it remained, for the most part, a slight and passing concern. The failure of the Labour party to recruit a large individual membership was a mark of this lack of interest. The problem lay not so much in a defective organization, as in the unimportant place which politics occupied in everyday life, the lack of any popular involvement in political activity except through the ballot box. Some historians have seen this relative indifference to political activity as an aspect of the declining level of popular participation in other kinds of local associations: churches, friendly societies, even sports clubs. In short, the British working class had little direct sense of community, outside work, and therefore displayed little political unity. Moreover, though work was an important source of common experiences, of 'class-consciousness', it did not create a solid and uniform class. While some of the divisions within the workforce had become less formidable since the war, others persisted and were even magnified. The gap between those with or without skills, receiving high or low wages, was somewhat diminished. On the other hand, the separation of the employed and the unemployed,

44

or those in irregular work, continued. The larger separation of the working population from those who did not work for wages – the old or married women – was if anything sharper. There was, in other words, no reason to expect the working class to share a single set of political attitudes, or conform to a single pattern of political behaviour. The Labour party might struggle to foster such solidarity, but it was struggling against considerable odds.

One further conclusion may be drawn from this analysis. We should probably not put much weight, in accounting for the patchiness of Labour's popularity, on the weaknesses of its own ideology and tactics. It is possible that the party's close identification with trade union interests was a liability in areas where industrial organization was slight, and even where it was more formidable but sectional in character. But it is not convincing to argue (as some left-wing critics of the party leadership suggested at the time) that a more radical and campaigning electoral appeal would have enjoyed greater success. Parties on the left – the Communists, formed in 1920, and the ILP after it split with the Labour party in 1932 – received only derisory support at elections. Labour had no difficulty in meeting their challenge, and arresting their progress. When it lost votes, at the peak of the inter-war depression, it lost them to the Conservative party and its allies. Disillusioned Labour supporters were far more likely to move a little to the right, politically, than to leap boldly to the left.

9

Economic policy and unemployment

Labour made most of its electoral gains, during the 1920s, as a party
of opposition. It was, however, always keen to show that it could
form an effective and popular government. For this reason, it twice
accepted office, in 1924 and 1929, even though it could command a
majority of MPs only if the Liberals gave the administration their
support. There were some critics on its own side who would have
preferred to avoid taking power on these conditions, since the party
would be prevented from carrying out its full programme, and in
particular from implementing socialist measures. But the judgement
of MacDonald and other leaders prevailed: that Labour would lose
support if it appeared afraid to govern the country; that the Liberals
might thereby be given a chance to re-establish their public standing;
and that a Labour administration, even if handicapped, could none
the less do something to safeguard the interests and improve the lot
of its own supporters.

This is precisely what the first Labour government, of 1924, set
out to accomplish. Since it could not contemplate the nationalization
of private industries or other forms of economic control by the
state, it concentrated much of its attention on social policy. Thus
it increased the rate of benefits paid to the unemployed and their
families, at the same time lessening their dependence on poor
law relief. It increased expenditure on public education, with
the leading objective of allowing more working-class children to
attend secondary schools. It introduced a housing act which offered
new government subsidies to local authorities who undertook to

build council dwellings. In addition, the Labour Chancellor, Philip Snowden, carried through a budget which removed various duties on imported foodstuffs, including sugar and coffee, so modestly reducing the cost of living.

These reforms were eminently cautious and moderate. They could not be thought financially extravagant. In fact, total public expenditure fell by more than £70 million between 1923 and 1924, thanks partly to smaller national debt charges and partly to declining military costs. Since the economy was recovering from the post-war depression during Labour's term of office, it could readily afford such additional outgoings. The government did not need to raise taxation, and probably did not wish to do so. It certainly frowned on borrowing money on a large scale, to pay for social services or any other item, for it saw this as involving the transfer of income from the tax-paying public at large to wealthy financiers and investors who held government bonds. Labour wished to establish its reputation for financial responsibility, and to see a complete return to prosperity, before it attempted anything more adventurous in the way of social reconstruction.

When it returned to power in 1929, its situation was not so happy. The Wall Street crash and the collapse of the American economy brought in its wake a rapid deterioration in international finance and trade. From the end of the year, Britain's unemployment rate began to rise. The monthly average of those registered as out of work increased from 1.2 million in 1929 to 1.9 million in 1930, and to 2.6 million in 1931. The cost of maintaining this labour reserve helped to push up public expenditure at a time when government income was stagnating or declining. As a result, the administration was faced by the problem of an unbalanced budget – government income falling short of current spending. By the early summer of 1931, a substantial financial deficit was being forecast. Subsequently, this was to play its part in a monetary crisis, as British and foreign investors lost confidence in the value of sterling as measured against other currencies.

The first, and the most fundamental, of these problems was unemployment. This had been a difficult question for the first Labour government too, but not then an urgent one. The unemployment rate was falling in 1924; and it was plausible to attribute the problem of the workless to the economic disruptions brought about by the war, which might become less severe as time passed. In 1929, this assumption was no longer credible. The persistence of an unemployment rate of about 10 per cent of the insured labour force pointed to some more deeply rooted weakness in the British economy. A party with working-class interests at heart could not afford to ignore this social incubus. Furthermore, the Liberals had, under Lloyd George's leadership, made this issue the centrepiece of their electoral campaign. Their pledge to 'conquer unemployment' clearly demanded a response from Labour, and placed the new cabinet, from the outset, under pressure to tackle this problem effectively. The pressure intensified as unemployment grew steadily worse.

For both Labour governments, and for the party in general, unemployment represented one of the evils of capitalism, for which the only permanent remedy was a socialist reconstruction of the economy. This did not mean, however, that high unemployment was accepted as inevitable under the present industrial regime. Capitalism had not given rise to it, at any rate persistently, before 1914, and it might reasonably be expected to perform better in the present. But such improvement in the condition of a market economy would, Labour concluded, require some help from the state. In the first place, according to Labour ministers, it required international co-operation between governments to restore normal conditions of trade. Since it was those industries with a large export market which were most depressed, and worst afflicted by unemployment, the revival of world commerce was obviously necessary to create jobs at home. This seemed to be the correct diagnosis both in 1924, when iron and steel and ship building were the trades in direst straits, and in 1929, when they had been joined by coal and textiles. Seen in this light, unemployment could be tackled by means of foreign policy. The first Labour administration sought to rectify the financial chaos which had resulted from the imposition of reparations upon Germany following the First World War. Its efforts helped to produce the 'Dawes plan', under which wartime debts were scaled down, and the USA agreed to make large international loans in order to support Germany's currency. MacDonald also did his best, though with less success, to re-establish trading relations between Britain and Russia, an enterprise of whose economic benefits the Labour movement had an altogether exaggerated notion. The Cabinet of 1929 pursued a similar line of policy. It threw its weight behind schemes for closer collaboration between different national banking systems, and tried to negotiate trading agreements with other countries that would prove helpful to British exporters. It took an active part in the economic conferences organized by the League of Nations. In 1930 it proposed and signed an international agreement which sought to arrest the general stampede towards protectionism by banning further additions to tariffs during the following year.

The other main plank of Labour's unemployment policy was the reorganization of industry. Since unemployment was concentrated in certain parts of the manufacturing sector, it appeared that the inefficiency and backwardness of British firms contributed to it. There were also grounds for believing that companies in this country were too small in comparison with their foreign rivals, and that competition between them was destructive. This analysis pointed to the desirability of what was fashionably termed 'rationalization': the amalgamation of smaller concerns, the elimination of the least productive, the renovation of equipment, co-operative measures between firms to facilitate exports, and so forth. Such policies could sometimes be effected by industrialists themselves; but on occasions the involvement of the government was thought necessary. The state could act as an intermediary in business negotiations; it could provide credit or arrange for the Bank of England to do so; it could legally enforce the agreements of industrialists to co-operate with one another. The Labour government considered intervention on these lines essential in the staple trades of cotton, iron and coal. It appointed official inquiries into the condition of the iron and cotton industries, and presided over complicated negotiations to carry out their recommendations. It introduced legislation for the coal industry in 1930, intended primarily to reduce the working day for miners, but establishing for the purpose production quotas and price controls. In addition, it took the first steps towards unifying the London passenger transport system under a public authority. In all these spheres it aimed to reduce cut-throat competition between private companies, and to bring about mergers or associations which would be able to plan investment, keep up prices and profits, and thus protect jobs.

Such moderate policies, enlisting support in business circles as much as within the Labour movement, were condemned by root-and-branch socialists. But the leaders of the party did not see them as inconsistent with socialism. Closer international ties, and a more highly centralized industrial system, signified for them a movement towards a socialist society. They made it easier to adopt collectivist policies in the future, and prepared public opinion for their reception. Politicians and trade unionists alike believed that socialism should be born of prosperity, not of economic adversity. Hence the Trades Union Congress, in the late 1920s, had approved industrial rationalization as fully as the Labour Cabinet. 'The approach to a new industrial order', wrote the TUC Secretary in 1927, 'is not by way of a social explosion, but by a planned reconstruction.'

Whether or not this programme could be defended in theory, however, its practical shortcomings were soon apparent. It conspicuously failed to provide a short-run answer to the unemployment problem. Striving for international economic partnership was admirable enough, but wholly futile in face of the determined nationalism of countries, new and old, many of whom were economically more depressed than Britain. As for rationalization, this was at best a long-drawn-out process, and whilst it might eventually make employment more secure, its adoption, especially in the staple export industries, might well create more unemployment initially. The closure of older factories and the installation of improved machinery allowed productivity to be increased but also allowed labour to be saved. Only when the demand for this industrial product expanded once more would there be any prospect of additional work – and this could not be expected amidst a world depression. Thus the Labour government had to cast around for other ways of solving the unemployment problem, more immediate in their effect.

MacDonald and his cabinet soon found that some of their own supporters desired a change of policy. They were heavily criticized by the left wing of the party, especially by the ILP. The latter had, in 1926, framed an economic strategy of its own, launched under the slogan, 'Socialism in our Time'. This had laid special emphasis on the desirability of raising the general level of wages, and other working-class income, holding that higher consumer spending in the home market would promote industrial recovery. The government did not take these proposals very seriously; and as the criticism of the ILP leadership became more strident, its influence diminished. More damaging was the discontent within the government itself, which was made public by the resignation of Oswald Mosley, one of the junior ministers responsible for unemployment policy, in May 1930. At the beginning of the year, Mosley had written a confidential memorandum attacking the Cabinet's present policies. He wanted a stronger government machine, more expenditure on immediate job creation schemes, and some tariff protection for industry, intending to expand the home market to offset the decline of British exports. Trade unionists were already becoming restive about the corollaries of rationalization, and at the Labour party conference in June Mosley received a good deal of popular backing. The government soon began to suffer reverses at by-elections, as its supporters in the country shared in the disillusionment.

What could the government do, however, to cut unemployment in the short run? Three policies were examined in 1930–1: the execution of a large programme of public works; the adoption of a more adventurous monetary policy; and the imposition of tariffs on imported goods. All of these found some advocates in the upper reaches of the labour movement. Those who, like Mosley, urged the remedy of public works, thought that substantial numbers of the out-of-work could be given jobs building roads, planting forests and extending the network of electricity supply. This had, in fact, been one of the ingredients of the party programme of 1918, though it had never been worked out with any precision. The reform of monetary policy was a proposal which Labour ministers could not understand so readily, and it was thus never very definitely formulated. In 1929, however, the government appointed a committee of inquiry, under Lord Macmillan, to examine the relations between the financial and industrial sectors, which was intended to give them a sense of direction in this *terra incognita*. As for the final policy option, the Cabinet held serious discussion on the possibility of agricultural protection throughout the spring and summer of 1930. At this stage their main concern was to defend British farmers against the 'dumping' of food surpluses from abroad. Thereafter, the government's attention was focused on another aspect of import duties: that of raising extra public revenue so as to meet rising government expenditure.

Eventually, none of these short-term policies was effectively pursued. The government did run a somewhat larger public works programme than its predecessor, but never gave work thereby to more than 6 or 7 per cent of those persons officially labelled as unemployed. It made arrangements for the banks to lend money to selected industries for the purposes of rationalization, but did not itself attempt any new or radical monetary policy, and it constantly deferred action on the issue of tariffs. More and more, in short, it gave the impression of helplessness and despair in face of the deepening economic crisis. Its natural inclination seemed to be to maintain relief benefits to the unemployed, and to wait for the economy to recover in its own time. It defended itself, in public, either by asserting that it had done all that it could in face of a world slump, or by claiming that the socialist measures which alone could combat unemployment were denied to it by the opposition parties.

What were the real reasons for the Labour administration's indecision? Could it, in fact, have accomplished more, in the way of counteracting the depression? On both these questions, historians disagree. Some lay blame on the government for its own deficiencies, and suggest that it was quite practicable for Britain to carry out the kind of constructive economic programme which was shortly to be enacted in the USA, as Roosevelt's 'New Deal'. On the other side, it is argued that there were many obstructions to the adoption of radical policies which the government could not ignore or overcome; and that, in any case, such policies had only a limited and gradual effect, even in America.

It is not likely that this disagreement will ever be fully resolved. Evidence can readily be found to support both points of view. On the one hand, it is clear that the Labour government, and the party as a whole, were ill-informed and disunited on important economic issues. There had been little detailed discussion on unemployment policy while Labour was in opposition during the 1920s. Only a handful of Labour politicians, even among the leadership, had any intellectual grasp of the complexities of financial and monetary policy. When in power, both the Cabinet and the wider movement were at odds over the merits of different short-term measures. A number of ministers, for example, including MacDonald himself, were very sceptical about the value of public works in combatting unemployment. Furthermore, the government, the party and the TUC alike were deeply split, in 1930–1, by the arguments for and against protection. The Cabinet, in short, could never identify any line of policy to tackle economic depression which commanded the general confidence and approval of ministers. Moreover its Chancellor of the Exchequer, Philip Snowden, took a conservative line in all these discussions. On tariffs, public works and financial questions, he took much the same conventional stance as his civil servants in the Treasury. Since he was definite and apparently knowledgeable, where others were uncertain and inexpert, his judgement prevailed.

It is possible, however, to present an interpretation of these economic reverses which places much less blame upon the Labour government. To begin with, MacDonald and his colleagues, when they set out to frame a short-term unemployment policy, encountered a series of difficulties which they could do little to overcome. These difficulties contributed to the government's own dissension. First, Labour ministers had to work with a civil service whose outlook on economic affairs was very conservative. The Treasury, especially, was averse to almost all radical initiatives. The Bank of England, which was still an independent corporation even if it worked closely with the state, expressed equally cautious opinions within its sphere. The government tried to correct the bias of the official establishment by appointing a new agency to make recommendations on economic questions: the Economic Advisory Council. But this body, from its establishment in 1929, proved as discordant as the Cabinet. It contained businessmen and trade unionists who predictably could not see eye to eye; but even the professional economists serving on it were found to be at loggerheads. To add to these problems, the government had also to try and reach agreement with the Liberal party on appropriate lines of action, in order to keep its majority in the Commons. While the Liberals had been determined enough on the conquest of unemployment at the 1929 election, they too grew more uncertain, however, and more distrustful of each other, during the next two years.

Seen in broader terms, the Labour government did not represent any large combination of radical forces in the country, which could have challenged the powerful conservative consensus that had always ruled economic policy. There was no extensive body of intellectual support for a distinct, left-wing economic programme. There was no body of public opinion; no pressure group outside the Labour movement, calling for a radical alternative; no discussion of novel ideas in the press. Nor were there, as yet, any foreign examples of bold new policy-making to suggest a model and encourage emulation – except, that is, for the five-year plan in Russia, whose character was little known and whose context was quite alien.

At the same time even those Labour leaders who, like Mac-Donald himself, were willing to seek new remedies for unemployment, were conscious of the danger of undermining business confidence. In an economic system that was still overwhelmingly under capitalist control, no policy could be pursued without regard to the response it would evoke among industrialists, financiers and investors. If businessmen were made to think that economic conditions were certain to grow worse, they would act in accordance with such expectations: cut back investment, close down more factories, dismiss workers or reduce their wages. If the government took no account of the state of business opinion, in other words, measures designed to remedy depression would render it more severe. It was primarily this consideration which led the Labour administration to prefer, wherever possible, to seek a wide spectrum of political support for its initiatives. In setting up the Economic Advisory Council and the Macmillan Committee, in drawing up plans for rationalization, eventually in trying to find a way out of the financial crisis of 1931, it sought for policies which would enjoy this general confidence. Thus it seemed, at times, to listen to its enemies more closely than its friends.

In the final analysis, we ought certainly to avoid finding the Labour government wholly innocent or guilty of abandoning the unemployed. Its culpability lay chiefly in its failure, before coming to power in 1929, to work out a clear and viable policy. Had it, from the outset, adopted an energetic and determined approach to the problem of unemployment, perhaps by undertaking extensive public works in combination with an expansionist credit policy, it might well have moderated the impact of the slump. But it had not made plans or preparations for such an effort. Instead, when it came into office, it pursued a strategy, based on international agreements and the rationalization of industry, which proved quite ineffectual. Once the commercial crisis began, however, it was far more difficult – perhaps actually impracticable – to devise and initiate a different set of measures. To say this, of course, is to lay the emphasis on the failure of Labour to draft adequate policies while in opposition. But in making this judgement, we should also remember that the party had only held power for one brief interval; and that it could not have anticipated the rapid decline in Britain's economic situation on its return to office. Before condemning the Labour administration too harshly, we should perhaps consider whether any other minority government, at this juncture, would have proved more capable.

10
The 1931 crisis and
the fall of the Labour government

The Labour government's failure to ease the burden of unemployment contributed largely, though indirectly, to its eventual collapse. In the summer of 1931, MacDonald and his colleagues were called on to deal with two urgent and related problems. The first was a large prospective budget deficit, the result of rises in public expenditure at a time when the economic slump was causing a fall in the receipts of taxation. The second was a rapid fall in Britain's reserves of gold and foreign currency, which resulted from the sale of sterling by large numbers of foreign bankers and financiers. The panicky behaviour of these foreign investors resulted partly from events elsewhere in the world, and in particular from the crash on the New York stock market in 1929 and the withdrawal of American financial assistance to Europe which followed upon it. But there was a connection between the two problems faced by the British government. The foreigners who sold their holdings of sterling were increasingly acting out of anxiety about the financial insolvency of the Labour ministry. When the Labour Cabinet sought to overcome its financial difficulties, however, it was unable to reach agreement; and on 23 August 1931 it submitted its resignation.

The government's budgetary problem arose particularly from the expense of maintaining a growing body of the unemployed. Their relief was furnished, in the first place, from an unemployment insurance scheme. First introduced in 1911, this had been extended in 1920 to cover the majority of wage-earners. By 1930, this scheme was itself in grave financial straits. The statutory contributions paid

55

by employers, workpeople and the state were becoming ever more insufficient to meet the costs of maintaining the out-of-work. The insurance debt grew from about £40 million in March 1930 to £75 million by March 1931.

A more serious matter for the Exchequer was that many of the unemployed no longer drew such insurance benefits, having been idle for too long to meet the qualifications. Their needs had to be met through a special, and supposedly temporary, 'transitional' benefit, for which the government itself furnished all the money. The ministry had increased its own liabilities, on this count, by permitting more people to claim such extraordinary relief. For much of the 1920s, insurance administrators had used various devices to disallow the claims of those unemployed whom they considered undeserving. In 1930, however, under pressure from the trade unions, the Labour government removed the most common ground for disqualification: the requirement that all recipients of benefits should prove they were 'genuinely seeking work'. Justified or not, this test had kept off the unemployment register many who were now readmitted. In the two months following its abolition, the number drawing transitional benefit rose from 140,000 to 300,000. For these and other reasons, public expenditure on unemployment assistance rose rapidly, from just under £4 million in 1929–30 to nearly £20 million in 1930–1.

The government's finances were stretched in other ways. Spending on roads and similar public works had been augmented during the depression. The demands of other social services, like education, were also higher, and the Treasury met more of the costs of local authorities. On the other hand, the government's revenue tended to stagnate or even to decline, since taxes on incomes and property yielded a lower return, and the consumption of alcohol and other articles carrying duties fell away. By the beginning of 1931 the Labour Chancellor, Snowden, was warning of a current deficit of some £40 million. By the following August, he was alarming his colleagues with predictions of an imbalance of some £170 million.

Not surprisingly, demands were issued in many quarters for cuts in public expenditure, especially on unemployment relief. Not only the opposition parties, and the National Confederation of Employers' Organizations, but the economists attached to the EAC urged, in the autumn and winter of 1930–1, that the rate of benefits to the out-of-work should be reduced. Furthermore, the Minister of Labour, Margaret Bondfield, took the same view, proposing a series of reforms to the Cabinet, from as early as May 1930,

56

designed to improve the finances of the scheme. The government steadily resisted such counsels, not least because it foresaw that measures of this kind would be condemned by the party and the movement. Even so, it seems certain that some ministers already felt that, eventually, cuts would be unavoidable. In October 1930, a Royal Commission on Unemployment Insurance was set up, and instructed to find means of balancing the books of the insurance scheme, and if necessary to make separate provision for the unemployed on transitional benefits. The inquiry was undertaken against the wishes of the TUC General Council, and without its participation. In June 1931, the Commission introduced an interim report, recommending immediate reductions in benefit.

What finally compelled the administration to address this issue, however, was the report, on 1 August 1931, of another committee, reviewing all areas of public expenditure. This had been appointed in February, under the chairmanship of an insurance magnate, Sir George May, in order to secure the support of Liberal MPs for new Treasury loans to the insurance fund. The majority of its members drew up an account of the national finances, far from dispassionate, which predicted public bankruptcy if retrenchment was not enforced. Forecasting a budget deficit of £120 million, they proposed a cut of 20 per cent in unemployment benefits, as well as the docking of teachers' and servicemen's salaries, the curtailment of the public works programme, and more assorted economies.

The importance of the May report arose from its appearance in the midst of a sterling crisis. In May 1931 a leading Austrian bank had declared itself insolvent; and subsequently many of its wealthy institutional customers had, to avoid the same fate, recalled the loans which they had made to other financial houses. As a result, in July 1931, the Bank of England found itself called on to repay many of its European creditors. It was, indeed, legally obliged to make these repayments in gold, or in whatever currency its clients desired, at a fixed rate of exchange – the 'gold standard'. The May Committee predicted that if the government did not correct its spendthrift ways it might be forced to devalue the pound. This prediction prompted more financiers and speculators to get rid of sterling. In the face of fears which spread through every important money market in the world, the government had to prove to the financial community that its budgetary affairs were in good order, in order to persuade bankers that they could safely hold on to their pounds.

An occasional voice was heard in the Labour movement advocating that the crisis should be met by devaluing the currency. The most important of these economic heretics was the union leader, Ernest Bevin. But the vast weight of informed opinion was set against this measure, which was never seriously contemplated by the Labour Cabinet. Ministers were told, with justification, that the abandonment of the gold standard would damage international trade, and thereby deepen the depression in Britain's export industries. They were also warned by the Chancellor, with quite unjustified exaggeration, that the effect would be to increase the price of imports and thereby raise the cost of living by half. The majority of the Cabinet judged, from ignorance, that such a step, unprecedented in peacetime, must have terrible consequences. They recalled the uncontrolled inflation which had occurred in Germany in 1923, when its currency had been undefended, and felt obscurely that the same danger awaited them. Advisers who, like the Governor of the Bank of England, thought public spending should be drastically cut, played upon these fears.

For ten days, in August 1931, members of the Labour Cabinet struggled to agree upon an emergency budget which would avoid devaluation. Most of them hoped, at the outset, that they could correct the financial deficit without cutting unemployment relief, by economising on other items of government expenditure, and by increasing taxes. This hope proved unrealistic. No budget would be enacted by Parliament unless approved by Liberal or Conservative MPs, and both the opposition parties were now united in insisting that unemployment benefit must be reduced. Furthermore, the French and American bankers who were asked for loans to help shore up the pound, indicated that all the parties in the Commons would be expected first to assent to measures of retrenchment. Ministers had no option but to consider lowering the level of unemployment relief. When they suggested this possibility to the TUC General Council and the Labour Party Executive, however, these bodies made clear their adamant opposition to this policy. Once they had taken such a stand, it was certain that a reduction of unemployment benefit would also be resisted by a substantial number of Labour MPs, and condemned by the sovereign party conference. Several ministers, of whom the most eminent was the foreign secretary, Arthur Henderson, concluded that it was preferable for the government to retire rather than to split the movement. The threat of collective resignation was sufficient to cause MacDonald to give up the struggle.

Some historians lean to the view that the Labour government was destroyed by its enemies: by the opposition parties and the bankers. This is what the party itself believed at the time, but while there is some truth in the suggestion that the Bank of England might have done more to avert the sterling crisis, it is the government's own limitations which seem chiefly responsible for its downfall. The administration was faced with economic problems to which, in the end, it could make only two responses. It might have accepted the devaluation of the pound, damning the consequences, but very few, if any, politicians were prepared to justify this course, even after the government's resignation. The alternative was to carry out the economies which would have balanced the budget, however obnoxious. This, it seems likely, is the decision which the Cabinet would have taken, had it not been for the objections which they met from the representatives of the labour movement, and especially from the General Council. The opposition of the union leaders to any significant cuts in official expenditure, and above all to the reduction of unemployment relief, proved decisive. It ensured that the Labour Cabinet itself could not agree on this course.

Why did the TUC spokesmen set themselves against economies, even though this entailed coming into conflict with Labour ministers and endangering the life of the government? The explanation lies partly in the unconvincing and limp fashion in which the Prime Minister and his Chancellor communicated their own view of the crisis. The TUC leaders were simply not persuaded that the economic circumstances justified the drastic change of policy proposed. This failure of understanding, however, reflected a lack of trust and cordiality between the two wings of the movement which can be traced back to the first Labour government. The unions had complained, then, of the reluctance of ministers to consult them, and had been angered by the manner in which the government had reacted to their use of the strike weapon. The TUC itself, over the next few years, displayed a strong desire to maintain its political independence, to enjoy the freedom to frame its own economic programme, and even to seek assistance outside the Labour party in getting it enacted. Its involvement in the 'Mond–Turner' talks of 1928–9 signalled this desire. The series of conferences thus named was arranged between trade unionists and large industrialists, led by a Conservative MP. The two sides discussed a wide range of policy issues, many of them concerned with action by central government: but the Labour party took no part.

The behaviour of the unions did not signify that they were consciously at odds with the party establishment – they continued to give it powerful support, and approved most of the programme on which it fought the 1929 election. Even when Labour was in power, the unions stood behind it when left-wing critics denounced its ineffectiveness. But there was no question that the TUC felt it had the right to express its own opinions and protect its own interests. This claim to autonomy was recognized in principle by Labour politicians; but its significance was not taken very seriously. MacDonald and his colleagues did not feel any urgent need to listen to the counsels and gauge the mood of the union leadership. In fact the Labour leadership, particularly when in office, was intent on dispelling the impression that it was merely the instrument of the union movement; and the unions, aware of this, were increasingly suspicious that their interests were being disregarded.

In 1931, accordingly, the General Council formed its own view of the crisis, and was unwilling to defer to that of the government. From the union standpoint, the cuts in public expenditure represented a breach of Labour's pledges to its working-class supporters. Worse than that, the proposed reductions in salaries and unemployment relief were considered to herald a general attack on wage standards, which many bankers and businessmen, and some economists, were known to favour. The TUC had, not surprisingly, consistently opposed this remedy for economic depression. It had stated, in November 1930, that it would prefer 'maintaining those unemployed and preserving the present standard of living for those in employment, rather than have unemployment eliminated immediately at the cost of a degradation in the standard of living of the workers'. Indeed, the general standard of living and unemployment benefits were seen as mutually dependent: an attack on the latter would entail a threat to the former. Union leaders believed, further, that a fall in wages or in benefits would worsen depression and unemployment, by lowering the demands of consumers for goods and services. Finally, some members of the General Council were, unlike the Cabinet, prepared to accept and even to welcome the abandonment of the gold standard. Its preservation, at the expense of Labour's social security programme, did not seem worth while.

The resignation of the Labour government precipitated the formation of a 'National' coalition, which Ramsay MacDonald consented to lead. We need not concern ourselves with his motives, for these did not influence the course of the party's development henceforth. From this perspective, it was only the fact of his departure which was important. This certainly had immediate repercussions on Labour's performance in the general election of October 1931. Its more lasting consequences are not easily discerned. What MacDonald's desertion did not effect, however, was a party schism. The fate of the Labour party in 1931 bears no resemblance to that of the Conservatives in 1846, or the Liberals in 1886 and 1916. This solidity of the party outside parliament reflected the strength which the trade unions gave to its organization, but it owed much to the fact that MacDonald himself made no attempt to carry any substantial support with him. He was joined in the National Government by three former colleagues: Snowden, Thomas and Lord Sankey. But he did not seek to enlist back-benchers, or to establish a rival party organization outside parliament. Twenty candidates only termed themselves 'National Labour' in the 1931 election, thirteen being returned. Since most of these relied upon the backing of the Conservatives, there was never any prospect of their becoming the nucleus of a separate political organization.

11
The 1931 election

The results of the election of October 1931 were catastrophic for the Labour party. It won only 46 seats, as compared with 288 in the 1929 election – although we may fairly add to this figure the six seats retained by ILP candidates, now standing independently. Its poll fell from 8.4 million to 6.5 million (or about 6.6 million if we include the ILP vote). As a proportion of all votes cast, its share declined from 37.1 per cent to 30.7 per cent. It was deprived of almost all its previous leadership: only one former Cabinet member, Lansbury, returned to the opposition benches, to become head of the party there. The rest of its MPs were composed largely of trade unionists, including 23 miners. And the party was to suffer further losses in the local government elections the following month.

Labour did so badly because it had no political leg to stand on. It could not make any plausible or coherent appeal to the electorate. It had been deserted by its most eminent leaders, including MacDonald. He now headed a National Government supported by Conservatives and Liberals alike, whose broad basis lent it a strong patriotic attraction. Labour's opponents painted a lurid and menacing picture of the economic disaster that would overtake all elements of society if the Socialists came back to office. For its part, the Labour party had no comprehensible alternative policy to the emergency financial measures which the National Government was now taking, but which it had previously failed to adopt.

Some historians have found it surprising that, faced by these odds, the Labour party did not suffer an even worse collapse. They emphasize the fact that the Labour and Socialist vote fell by only a little more than 6 per cent, and they conclude that the humiliation which the party suffered was primarily due not to the desertion of its working-class supporters, but to the unity of the opposition. In 1929, Liberals and Conservatives fought each other across the country. In 1931 there were far fewer Liberals in the field – 159 as opposed to 513. The number of election contests involving more than two adversaries thus fell from 449 in 1929 to 99 in 1931. Most of the votes which the Liberals had formerly attracted now went to the Conservatives; where Liberal candidates withdrew, it has been estimated that three in five of their former electorate rallied to the Tories, while only one transferred to Labour. At the same time, 74 Liberals received Conservative support. Just as Labour had gained seats by forming a tacit alliance with the Liberals before 1914, so it now lost heavily when an alliance was arrayed against it.

We cannot, however, explain the outcome of the 1931 election without drawing attention again to the numbers of working-class votes cast *against* the Labour party. If we ignore the minor parties, some 14.6 million electors were ranged against Labour, who could muster only 6.6 million on its side. Even if the vast majority of Labour's electorate were working class, it must still be concluded that around ten million wage-earners, of some description, voted for the candidates of the National coalition. The political crisis emphatically confirmed the attraction, in British society, of the kind of moderate, undogmatic and mildly patriotic Conservatism represented by Stanley Baldwin. In this country, economic instability brought no accession of support to radical parties and novel ideologies, as it did in Germany, and later in France and Spain. Neither the Communists nor the 'New Party' of Oswald Mosley achieved a significant poll in 1931. The crisis produced a violent swing of the old political pendulum, but did not stop the clock.

If we look closely at the character and consequences of the slump, we can readily understand its political outcome. We have seen already that the working class was not widely or firmly attached to a Labour movement. The trade unions had been losing membership since 1924. The depression which began in 1929 did not raise class-consciousness. Unlike that of the early 1920s, it was not associated with widespread strikes and lockouts. Indeed, since wage cuts were quite rarely imposed and never severe, most of those workers who kept their jobs were by no means discontented with their material well-being. In such circumstances, they had something to lose. The economic crisis was, for them, readily

63

bearable; it might, however, get much worse. A working-class audience was thus well-prepared to listen to the alarming stories told by National Government leaders about the disaster which would ensue if Labour returned to office. They were also, perhaps, responsive to the Conservative promise that tariff protection would prevent any further economic deterioration. Only in areas where unemployment and poverty were especially concentrated, like the slums of Glasgow and East London, or in those where dislike of Conservatism was particularly marked, like the South Wales coalfield, was this propaganda ineffective.

Devastating as it was, the 1931 election left the organization of the Labour party largely intact. There were, indeed, some aspects of the defeat from which the party could take comfort. It represented a further stage in the simplification of the party system into a direct confrontation between Labour and the Conservatives. After the crisis, a substantial body of the Liberals, under Sir John Simon, formed a permanent alliance with the Tories. Any public reaction against Conservative policies and government was now still more likely to help Labour, as the only visible opposition. The crisis also restored the political alliance between Labour and the trade unions. The latter were aware of the need to prevent any future rift between themselves and the party leadership, of the kind which had appeared in 1931. They showed their anxiety to play a more active role in preparing and publicizing party policies. Finally, the next generation of Labour leaders acquired, in many instances, a better understanding of the difficulties of exercising power. The more clear-sighted and realistic outlook of the Labour government elected in 1945 was not simply the product of the failures of 1929–31, but those failures none the less played a part in its preparation.

12
Conclusion

The Labour party had, during the period of thirty years or so covered by this study, experienced a remarkable advance. It had set up a national political organization of a new kind, which had proved both flexible and durable. It had greatly increased its electoral support, overtaking and almost destroying its Liberal rival. It had formulated and publicized a distinctive programme, resting upon a creed which aroused much enthusiasm and dedication, and it twice took on, under difficult conditions, the responsibilities of government. Its achievements on the first two counts were, admittedly, greater than on the third and fourth. Yet while doing little to demonstrate the practicality of its socialist faith, it played its part in sustaining a form of democratic and parliamentary government which, elsewhere in Europe, proved vulnerable and fragile.

The Labour party's popular following had manifestly little to do with its presumed or proven capacity to govern. Yet the electors who flocked to it were not simply registering a political protest against the older parties. Before the First World War, it is true, they had no expectation that Labour would gain office. Within a few years of the end of war, however, such a ministry was a realistic prospect, from which Labour voters might expect concrete benefits. The party had, in short, secured recognition as a potential party of government. In so doing, it owed something to the obvious success with which its representatives had adapted to the conventions and practices of parliamentary life, and something to the inclusion of a few of its leaders in the wartime administrations of Asquith and Lloyd George. Its right to enjoy access to power was acknowledged, for different reasons, by the Conservatives and the Liberals. In addition, Labour's competence seemed assured, not just by virtue of the moderation of its 'socialist' policies, but because they bore a significant resemblance to measures already carried out by other parties. The war had appeared to demonstrate the feasibility of economic regulation and state enterprise. The social reforms of the Liberals before 1914 and of the Coalition after 1918 demonstrated the possibilities of large-scale public welfare. Labour was not promising anything radically new, but simply the more complete and determined implementation of policies already tried and experienced. There seemed no reason why it should not accomplish what was so familiar.

If voters, new and old, flocked to the Labour party after 1918, however, it was not from any specific attraction to the content of its policies, but from an indefinite sense that it was to be trusted, better than other parties, to safeguard their interests. It was this feeling, of instinctive and unquestioning allegiance, which marked what is termed 'the growth of class politics'. For the greater part of the nineteenth century, political parties had sought to base themselves on social solidarities of a more local character, and to enlist the support of those local notables who were the natural leaders of their communities. If they appealed to a wider audience, it was through the medium of religious associations or moral pressure groups. By the 1880s and 1890s, however, a trend to a new pattern could already be observed. Increasingly, the Liberal party sought to appeal to the 'labour' interest, and the Conservatives expressed the opposing interests of property in all forms. The electoral strength of the one came to lie predominantly in working-class areas; that of the other, though less exactly, in rural and middle-class constituencies. The formation of the Labour party can thus be seen as the outcome and extension of this trend. Its success reflected the advance of class voting, which reached its furthest limit, outside our period, in 1945–51. Since then, the nature of electoral behaviour has gradually altered; and the debate over policy within the Labour party of the present day is to an extent the reflection of that change. In its early life, however, the party could rest its electoral appeal, with confidence, on its claim to understand working-class needs and aspirations.

We must be careful, however, to qualify these generalizations. The Labour party was set up, in 1900, not so much as the instrument of the working class as of the trade unions. Its rapid progress resulted, directly or indirectly, from the fact that it incorporated organizations, powerful and wealthy, that were already in being. It was always to remain a federal structure, containing the unions, and later the co-operatives, as autonomous bodies, demanding the loyalty of their own members, and with their own functions and purposes. From the party's viewpoint, this union backing was essential, but it was never sufficient to ensure electoral success. The trade unions could not guarantee that all their own members would vote Labour, still less that the majority of working-class electors outside their ranks would do so. Labour might aspire to attract the allegiance of a whole class, but such an achievement was far beyond it.

In viewing Labour as a working-class party, moreover, it should be remembered that the leadership did not wish it to be simply a vehicle of class interests. At least after the adoption of a party programme in 1918, they hoped to gain a wider following. Socialist ideas had, in fact, always exercised an attraction for some members of the middle class. In addition, Labour inherited some of the religious and moral traditions of Liberalism. It is unlikely that, prior to 1931, the party won a significant vote outside the ranks of the wage-earning population, but the fact that it hoped to do so influenced its behaviour, especially during the two periods when it held office. Hence it was subject to internal conflict over whether it should ignore or override the immediate interests of its union constituents (and many of its own voters) in the name of a greater national good, and of some larger and more distant goal or ideal. This, indeed, can be seen as a perennial problem for Labour administrations. There are parallels, for instance, between the first Labour government's disapproving attitude to industrial disputes in 1924, and the views of its latest successor upon the 'winter of discontent' in 1978–9. On both occasions, Labour ministers recognized that they had to maintain public services, even if this entailed weakening the impact of industrial stoppages. There was a similar resemblance between the efforts of the government of 1929 to maintain the gold standard, and the adherence of the ministries of the 1960s and 70s to the strict financial policies demanded by the International Monetary Fund. In all these crises, a socialist administration found itself justifying cuts in welfare spending for the sake of monetary and financial stability. This is not, of course, to say that every Labour government must lead to a debacle like 1931, but it should not be found surprising that Labour governments have so frequently failed to please the party and the electorate which they ostensibly represent.

Further reading

Place of publication is London unless otherwise stated.

There are several general histories of the Labour party which cover the period from 1900 to 1931. One of the more recent is R. Moore's *The Emergence of the Labour Party, 1900–24* (Hodder & Stoughton, 1978), while Henry Pelling's *Short History of the Labour Party* (Macmillan, 8th edition), was last updated in 1985. A concise account, heavily reliant on Pelling's work, is provided by Paul Adelman's *The Rise of the Labour Party, 1880–1945* (Longman, 1972). G. D. H. Cole's *The History of the Labour Party since 1914* (Routledge, 1948) is a good deal older, but still retains value, in part because of Cole's intimate involvement with the affairs of the labour movement. An important work by Duncan Tanner, *Political Change and the Labour Party, 1900–1918* (Cambridge University Press, Cambridge, 1990) contains a complex and novel interpretation, which lays great stress on the influence of local conditions on the fortunes of competing parties, and hence on the uneven pace of Labour's electoral advance. Though its detailed analysis ends in 1918, the concluding chapter offers a survey of the inter-war years.

A somewhat broader perspective, treating the Labour party as an element of the Labour movement, or of the history of the working class, is to be found in R. Hinton, *Labour and Socialism: A history of the British Labour Movement, 1867–1974*, (Wheatsheaf, Brighton, 1983), and more discursively in R. Price, *Labour in British Society* (Croom Helm, 1986) and J. E. Cronin, *Labour and Society, 1918–79* (Batsford, 1984). The role of the trade unions in the development of the party is fully discussed in H. A. Clegg, A. Fox and A. F. Thompson, *A History of British Trade Unions since 1889*, vol. 1, and H. A. Clegg's second volume, under the same title, carrying the story from 1910 to 1933 (Clarendon Press, Oxford; 1964 and 1985). The best accounts of the relations between the Labour party and Socialist organizations deal only with the years before 1914: David Howell, *British Workers and the Independent Labour Party* (Manchester University Press, Manchester, 1983), and S. Pierson, *British Socialists: the Journey from Fantasy to Politics* (Harvard University Press, Cambridge, Mass., 1979). J. Z. Young, *Socialism and the English working class* (Harvester–Wheatsheaf, Brighton, 1989) is interesting, but somewhat repetitious.

A more specialized study of party development is to be found in Ross McKibbin, *The Evolution of the Labour Party, 1910–1924* (Oxford University Press, Oxford, 1974). An important collection of essays, *The First Labour Party*, edited by K. D. Brown (Croom Helm, 1985), contains contributions dealing with the period before the First World War. Other essays, of more varied character, may be found in D. E. Martin and D. Rubinstein (eds.), *Ideology and the Labour Movement* (Croom Helm, 1979).

The electoral fortunes of Labour can be traced in some detail in works which deal with the election of 1906 (A. K. Russell, *Liberal Landslide*: David & Charles, Newton Abbot, 1973); that of 1910 (Neil Blewett, *The Peers, the Parties and the People:* Macmillan, 1972); and those of 1918–29 (Chris Cook, *The Age of Alignment: Electoral Politics in Britain, 1922–29*: Macmillan, 1975). For the 1931 election, the work of John Stevenson and Chris Cook, *The Slump* (Jonathan Cape, 1977), may be consulted.

Some good biographies of Labour leaders contain much information about the development of the party as a whole. This is particularly true of David Marquand's *Ramsay MacDonald* (Jonathan Cape, 1977), *Arthur Henderson*, by F. M. Leventhal, (Manchester University Press, Manchester, 1989), and K. O. Morgan's *Keir Hardie* (Weidenfeld & Nicolson, 1975).

Local and regional investigations of the Labour party furnish case studies which are needed to indicate the variety of the national pattern. The best of them, like Michael Savage's *The Dynamics of Working Class Politics: The Labour Movement in Preston, 1880–1940* (Cambridge University Press, Cambridge, 1987), contain a much broader interpretation of Labour's growth. Other recent works in this category include Jack Reynolds and Keith Laybourne, *Labour Heartland: The History of the Labour Party in West Yorkshire during the Inter-war Years* (Bradford University, Bradford, 1987), David Clark, *Colne Valley: Radicalism to Socialism* (Longman, 1981), and I. Donnachie, C. Harvie and I. Wood (eds), *Forward. Labour Politics in Scotland, 1888–1988* (Polygon, Edinburgh, 1989). Ian Maclean's *The Legend of Red Clydeside* (John Donald, Edinburgh, 1983) offers an interesting analysis of Labour electoral advance in the Glasgow area, which also has wider relevance.

The history of the Labour governments of this period is treated by R. W. Lyman, *The First Labour Government* (Chapman, 1957), now rather out of date, and Robert Skidelsky, *Politicians and the Slump* (Penguin, Harmondsworth, 1970). Other aspects of the party's policy making can also be studied, thanks to K. D. Brown, *Labour and Unemployment, 1900–1914* (David & Charles, Newton Abbot, 1971), and W. R. Garside, *British Unemployment, 1919–39*, (Cambridge University Press, Cambridge, 1990), especially Part IV. There are also some useful essays on Labour economic policy in Alan Booth and Melvyn Pack, *Employment, Capital and Economic Policy: Great Britain 1918–39* (Blackwell, Oxford, 1985).

There are documentary collections which enable some aspects of party history to be looked at through contemporary sources: Henry Pelling, *The Challenge of Socialism* (A. & C. Black, 1954), Frank Bealey, *The Social and Political Thought of the British Labour Party*, (Weidenfeld & Nicolson, 1970) and for the period leading up to the party's foundation, Eric Hobsbawm, *Labour's Turning Point* (first published by Lawrence & Wishart in 1948, and reprinted by Harvester, Brighton, in 1974).